HEALING FOR YOUR BROKEN HEART

James and Lyn Kirkland

Messianic & Christian Publisher

Published by
Olive Press צהר זית
Messianic and Christian Publisher
P.O. Box 163
Copenhagen, NY 13626

Messianic & Christian Publisher

Our prayer at Olive Press is that we may help make the Word of Adonai fully known, that it spread rapidly and be glorified everywhere. We hope our books help open people's eyes so they will turn from darkness to Light and from the power of the adversary to God and to trust in ישוע Yeshua (Jesus). (From II Thess. 3:1; Col. 1:25; Acts 26:18,15 NRSV and CJB, the *Complete Jewish Bible*)
May this book in particular help bring healing to those with inner wounds.

In honor to God, pronouns referring to the Trinity are capitalized, satan's names are not. But not all Bible versions do this and legally must be printed as they are.

www.olivepresspublisher.com

Cover and interior design by Olive Press.
Cover butterfly photo © 2012 by Allan Miller
Cover broken heart images © 2012 by Shutterstock.com

Healing For Your Broken Heart

Copyright © 2012 by James and Lyn Kirkland

All rights reserved. No part of this book may be reproduced, stored in a retrieval system, or transmitted in any way by any means—electronic, mechanical, photocopy, recording, or otherwise—without the prior permission of the copyright holder, except as provided by USA copyright law.

ISBN 978-0-9847111-4-7
Printed in the USA.
1. Christian Inspirational 2. Christian Spiritual Growth 3. Body, mind, & spirit: healing: prayer & spiritual

To avoid copyright issues, all but a couple Scriptures are taken from the *King James Version* of the Bible.

Verses marked NKJV are taken from the New King James Version. Copyright © 1982 by Thomas Nelson, Inc. All rights reserved.

Verses marked NLT are taken from the The Holy Bible, New Living Translation. Copyright © 1996, by Tyndale House Publishers, Inc., Wheaton, IL 60189 USA. All rights reserved.

TABLE OF CONTENTS

Part 1: Effective Coping Methods

Chapter 1: The Beginning of the End   11
Explains briefly Lyn's personal story of betrayal, initial reactions, and beginning survival methods

Chapter 2: Give Yourself to God   13
Details the comfort derived from placing oneself totally into the Lord's arms

Chapter 3: Seek Professional Help   16
Recommendation to seek emotional assistance from a trained counselor or therapist

Chapter 4: A Network of Angels   18
Explains how sharing the hurt with family/friends allows them to help heal one's wounded spirit

Chapter 5: Keeping Busy   21
How decision to fill one's time with some activities can have positive results

Chapter 6: Wake-Up Call   24
Eventually using the event as opportunity for self-evaluation and improvement

Chapter 7: Nature As A Healing Source   26
How experiencing and appreciating God's creation can bring peace and healing

Chapter 8: Keeping A Journal   28
Explains the benefits of releasing inner turmoil by writing one's innermost thoughts and feelings on paper

Chapter 9: Warning Signs   31
Re-evaluation of events allows one to see the situation from a new perspective

Chapter 10: Make A Plan For The Future   33
Choosing values, recognizing self-worth, and planning courageously to step into the future

Part 2: Spiritual Healing

Chapter 11: Who God Is   43
Reveals the goodness and love of God as set forth in the Scriptures. Likewise, Scriptural knowledge on how to recognize the enemy, satan

Chapter 12: Who You Are In Christ   50
Addresses the pain of feeling "valueless" and counteracts that pain with a Scriptural summary of our worth in Christ

Chapter 13: Faith vs. Fear   60
How to exercise and strengthen our faith as part of God's plan, while moving out of satan's plan for us to live in fear

Chapter 14: Traps   67
How to be prepared to counteract the traps (i.e. self pity, hopelessness, anger, replay) satan will try to inflict

Chapter 15: Forgiveness   70
Scriptural explanation of forgiveness; ten practical steps to obtain victory and healing that come from choosing to forgive

Chapter 16: How to Pray   75
God has made a way for us to pray effectively to defeat satan's attacks. This chapter details how your faith combined with speaking Scripture conquers the devil's plans

Appendix
Scripture Verses of Encouragement and Hope   81

INTRODUCTION

One of the more shocking and unfortunate truths of the end times in which we live is the fact that the divorce rate in America is approaching 60%. What may be even more shocking is that the divorce rate among Christian couples is approaching the same figure. What is it about our world that would make such a thing true? What causes people who must have loved each other at one time, and who made vows that they must have taken seriously at the time, abandon them and their Christian principles with little or no regard for anyone but themselves? II Timothy 3 provides us with some insight into the characteristics of end times Christians, listing at least eighteen prominent character traits that will be prevalent in the end times. First on the list is that "men shall be lovers of their own selves". That is, the most prominent characteristic of end time Christians is selfishness.

A study of Godly love in the New Testament will reveal the basic truths that love, as Christ lived it and taught it, is characterized by giving rather than receiving, and is directed toward others rather than self. In the world in which we find ourselves, these characteristics are becoming more and more rare. They are being replaced by an emphasis on self that is so overwhelming that solemn promises before God, such as marriage vows, are being rationalized away.

This book is being written by two Christians who have experienced the shock and pain of marital betrayal after 26 years of married life. It is not just a survival manual, but a blueprint for victory. The book is divided into two sections; the first describes a series of coping mechanisms designed to guide the victim of marital betrayal through the difficult adjustment period immediately following the discovery of the betrayal (almost always, this occurs without warning). The second section addresses some of the most important areas on the road to spiritual healing and victory over this devastating event.

Yes, healing is not only a possibility, but is promised by God Himself. And yes, we speak of victory, not as something merely hoped for, or wished for, but as something that we know by experience can be a reality.

Furthermore, this book applies not only to marital betrayal, but to betrayal in any relationship. The principles are the same; the pain and devastation are no less severe; and the need for help is no less real. Our prayerful goal is that you might experience the sweet victory that CAN be realized through faith in the Word of God and it's Author.

PART 1

EFFECTIVE COPING METHODS

(Author's note: The chapters in Part 1 were written by Lyn immediately following her ex-husband's betrayal. They were written in present tense and have been left in that tense so as to better identify with you, the reader.)

Chapter 1

The Beginning of the End

I thought my life ended the day my husband, Edward, told me that he didn't love me any more and wanted to leave me. For 26 years, I had been married to Ed. I was contented…I often exclaimed how lucky I was. I truly thought we had a good relationship and were happy with each other. But in an instant, this happy life changed to one of pain and bewilderment.

I suppose there is no easy way to tell the person you've been married to for 26 years that you want to leave. In my case, my husband blurted out those words as we were preparing for a Saturday evening visit with our friends. I felt as though I was in a dream. This wasn't really happening to me…..this *couldn't* be happening to me!

I pleaded with him to tell me what was wrong and why he had made such a statement. Ed was always so considerate and caring of my feelings, but he responded to my panic in a most uncharacteristic way. He matter-of-factly said he thought I would have seen it coming—that we had been drifting apart for a while, and that he had been wanting to tell me for quite some time. I felt terror like I've never known. I told him we could "fix" whatever he felt was wrong. The intense ache was the worst pain I have ever known. I died inside myself that day—the one I loved more than myself and trusted with my very life had betrayed and hurt me in a way unimaginable. As I look back on that evening (and the next few days and weeks), it's all a blur. My initial reaction was to ask for details…..HOW could this happen….WHY was it happening….WHAT could we do to make it go away? I felt as though I was hit by a truck, that my heart would leap out of my chest. My throat was dry, my head was spinning, my stomach sick….this had to be a dream, a nightmare from which I would certainly wake up.

I laid in bed and cried for the next two days. The only time I got up was to call a marriage counselor chosen randomly from the

Part 1

yellow pages of the phone book and set an appointment for Monday (two days away). Slowly over those next two days, the details of his story of betrayal emerged. He and a co-worker had become attracted to each other, and this attraction emerged into an affair that had been going on for the past year. As I tried to absorb the facts, my heart ached so agonizingly, I couldn't imagine how I was going to endure this pain. I set my sights on the planned visit to the marriage counselor, somehow lulling myself into the false expectation that once the marriage counselor met with us and heard our story, she would begin the steps to make everything better. After attending only three sessions together, Ed announced that he would not be returning to the therapist. His heart was set on leaving, and that was that. I think that's when reality hit me…our marriage was in severe trouble. I couldn't deny it any longer or fall back on false hope. My eyes were finally opened to the inevitable.

And so, in my heart and in my head, I now knew what was so evident. I had not told another living soul about my crisis (other than my marriage counselor). I knew I wasn't fooling myself, but I could hardly think about my situation, much less verbalize it to anyone else. Now what was I going to do? I did not yet possess the presence of mind to formulate a plan for coping or recovery….I simply was not ready or capable of sharing the pain. I was still reeling with disbelief. The one and only conscious decision I did make was to place myself in the hands of God. And so, as a child runs to her mother for safety and solace, I spiritually and emotionally flung myself into God's arms. And there, my friends, is where I remained.

In the following chapters, I will explain how, with God's help, I survived. The human spirit is truly strong. I am living proof. The anguish of betrayal is a very painful cross to bear. I hope that by sharing my methods of coping with this tragedy, I may help others who will also travel this road. We are soulmates, those of us who are bound together by this common suffering. Let us draw strength from one another, hold each other's hand, and survive together.

Chapter 2

Give Yourself To God

As a Christian, I see and feel the presence of God in my life. I learned to pray and trust in God as a child from the example set by my parents, and the gift of faith has been an integral part of my life. Because of this gift, I knew no other response to my woundedness than to turn to God for comfort. Alone, I could not handle the severity of the pain and injustice that had become so all encompassing in my life. The sense of abandonment by my husband did not cause me to question God or blame Him. No, it prompted me to rely on God for protection, guidance, love, and healing. Faith cannot be explained, it can only be felt. In the depths of my heart, I knew that although I may be forsaken by all others, even the one human being I loved most of all, God would NEVER forsake me.

My constant thought was "God help me." I imagined myself being picked up and carried by a strong, calm, warm pair of arms. I allowed myself to be comforted by this mental image. I could not even form the words to pray…my mere plea for help to God was all I could utter for the first few days. And God heard my plea. I knew there was no way I could survive on my own. My mind kept hearing those comforting words in the Bible, "He has carved you on the palm of His hand." It is in God's hands that I began to learn to endure. I asked Him to show me how to live on, and He helped me to begin. I knew I would never be the same again, but I began to discover how to be strong. Sometimes I did not want to be strong…I just wanted to be held and taken care of. It was at those times that God carried me. Life can be hard sometimes, and I had certainly hit hard times. The ache I felt inside did not go away, and I wondered if I would ever be able to trust again. It was too soon to know, but not too soon to think about my future…a future that I had placed in God's hands. Some days I made no progress, but always felt the security of being loved by the Being who had created me. There was comfort in knowing that my faith was sustaining me. I had lost a part of my heart, a part of me that used to exist. Maybe someday I would find happiness in my heart again. For the time being, I would be content to hear my heart beat and watch my new life take shape – bit by tiny bit, surviving by the grace of God.

I made a vow that prayer would continue to be a part of my daily life. Some days, it was the only conscious effort I can remember making. As the reality of my "aloneness" sank in, my times of prayer were a comfort to me. Each night before I went to sleep, I folded my hands and closed my eyes, and pictured God waiting to comfort His child. I read the Bible, and sometimes read from a book given to me by a friend which provides a daily meditation and prayer. It was not accidental how many times the meditation coincided with my thoughts or mood that day. In my mind, that was just one more indication that God indeed was with me every moment of every day. My daily thought was "God is carrying me in the palm of His hand."

At first, attending church alone was a bit intimidating... people would wonder where Ed was. (I told them at the time that he was away on a trip with his Military Reserves Unit.) This response bought me some time and was a reasonable explanation, as I protected myself from innocent questions. Everyone knew Ed had been in the Reserves for the past 18 years and frequently was sent on special flying missions. Little did my fellow church members know how difficult it was for me to sit in the pew alone while trying desperately to appear "normal". I felt like nothing would ever be normal in my life again. Once more, I became aware of the calming effect prayer had on my heart and spirit. Nothing about our situation had changed, but in my heart, acceptance was beginning to grow. The fear of my future and a subliminal need for "a plan to retaliate" began to be overcome by a prayerful resolution to maintain my dignity and charity (a feat impossible by mere human resolve). Once again, God was working His small miracles within me.

You do not need to be a religious person to pray, nor do you need to go to a church to pray. All that is necessary is a sincere plea from the heart..."God help me!" God hears the smallest, weakest murmur from the depths of the most desolate being. Don't ask for specifics; don't question, promise, or barter. Simply place yourself in His care and allow yourself to be comforted. It may not happen immediately, but if you trust, you will be helped. Faith grows from the tiniest seed. Allow yourself to trust in God. He will not forsake you!

Note: Please refer to Chapter 11 in Part 2 of this book for a Scriptural explanation of WHY you CAN put your trust in God.

Chapter 3
Seek Professional Help

The only experience I had ever had in my life with a professional counselor was with the Guidance Counselor at my children's school for study aid and helping to overcome shyness. What I was experiencing now was a far cry from those subjects. Lacking the expertise to begin to address this crisis, I had absolutely no hesitation in contacting a therapist for help. I opened the phone book to the yellow pages, began to read over the 100-plus names, bowed my head and simply asked God to lead me to the right one. It could only have been the hand of God that guided me to call my therapist, Susanne.

I was almost panic-stricken when I made that call. It was the weekend, and I was positive that I would dial into voice mail or an answering service. I really have no recollection of the words I used, but I'm sure my quivering voice was an indication of my emotional state at the time of that initial phone call. Miraculously, the therapist, Susanne, called me back within two hours (her voice mail message did say that she checked her messages often). I was extremely relieved at her quick response to my message.

She was compassionate, calming, and professional, and after speaking with her briefly to set an appointment, I knew I had just taken my first step to take control of my life. As I mentioned previously, Ed and I attended only three sessions of marriage counseling together when Ed announced he would not be returning. I think we were getting too close to the real issues, and he was not prepared or willing to share his feelings with a therapist or me. However, from that point on, I made the decision that I would attend counseling sessions alone (not for marriage counseling, but for individual counseling). Susanne assured me that together we would formulate a plan for my coping with my life's change. I continued my weekly one-hour sessions with my therapist, and Susanne became a very important part of my life. I have shared with her every detail of my pain, and we have delved into every aspect involved with this trauma. She is helping me to be strong, and although it is far from easy, it is a healing experience, and I have come to look forward to our weekly sessions. She has become a friend to me, and I know she cares about me. I am fortunate to have found such a competent, caring, and skilled counselor who is an important part of my survival.

In addition to my therapist, I also have a spiritual director, the former assistant pastor at the church I attended. He has maintained a friendship with my family for 14 years and has been my spiritual director during those years. Since my faith is an integral part of who I am and how I cope, it was only natural that I share this life trauma with him. He has been the Lord's helper to heal my soul throughout this experience. With prayer, guidance, and spiritual direction, I have kept in touch with God in a very special way while experiencing this painful journey.

Just as a person who is physically ill needs care and treatment from a physician, one who is emotionally afflicted need professional care, also. I urge you to seek help from a qualified counselor and/or spiritual director. These trained professionals are a source of healing and solace for your spirit. If you do not feel your choice of therapists is a "good fit", seek help from another. I was fortunate in that the cost of my therapy was covered nearly completely by my employer health plan. However, there are social and church agencies that provide emotional support and counseling on a sliding pay scale. Do not be embarrassed or fearful to seek their aid. Emotional pain should not be borne alone…unburden your pain and fears to one who has been trained to help. This is one more way to begin to heal the devastation created by betrayal.

Chapter 4

A Network of Angels

For the first few weeks after my spouse admitted his betrayal and decision to leave me, I must admit that I was too shocked and stunned to properly anticipate the changes that would occur in myself. My thoughts about the future were anxious and pessimistic. I had to concentrate on just getting through each day, each hour. Except for discussing my emotional loss with my therapist and spiritual advisor, I told no one any details. I had no appetite and felt sick most of the time. I began to lose weight because I was not eating properly. My co-workers and family members began to question me about my health, and I said that I was experiencing stomach problems. I simply was not able to tell anyone else about Ed's actions and our subsequent separation.

Most of the time I felt grief-stricken, exhausted, and drained. My heart was still aching so agonizingly, I wasn't sure how I could bear this anguish. But somewhere in the back of my heart, I must have believed that if I told no one, the truth was not real. And so, I kept the story of my marital troubles from my friends and family, hoping against hope that one day soon Ed would tell me he had made a big mistake, and we would get back together and try to make our marriage work.

The effort involved in this cover-up was beginning to take its toll on me. My boss and co-workers, sisters, parents, and children (ages 23 and 26, living away from home) began to question me about my health. I was growing weary of making up stories, and so I made the decision to begin telling those people closest to me about what happened. I started with my children, my three sisters (one by one), and my parents. Then I told my boss, co-workers, and closest friends. They allowed me to talk and express what I was feeling, without interrupting, judging, or censoring my words and feelings.

Although extremely painful, I found it to be a freeing experience each time I told someone. The love, kindness, and understanding from family members and friends was truly heartwarming. I wasn't strong or noble…I was grief-stricken and angry! They didn't claim to know how I was feeling, didn't try to "fix" me, or make me all better. They listened, cared for, and stood by me for as long as I needed to talk. They have continued to call and care for me, invite me to dinner, send me cards, and offer other gestures of support and kindness.

I encountered much anxiety over sharing with my children the betrayal by their father. I vowed to say or do nothing that would make them feel as though they were put in the middle. Although they are grown up, they are still my children, and I wanted to protect them from hurt. I began to agonize over the effect this trauma would cause in their lives. A dear friend knew how much pain this worry was causing me, and gently advised me to begin to look at the situation from a different point of view. She suggested that my children and I make a promise to help each other work through this turn in our lives together, rather than me trying to "make it better" for my children. This suggestion lifted a great weight from my shoulders. It was one more step taken, and another indication of the love and care my dearest friends were showing me.

As painful as it may be, I gently urge you to consider taking the steps to share your pain with your family and friends, if possible. God made us social beings, and it is not healthy to isolate yourself and try to bear your loss on your own. Allow yourself permission to accept small acts of kindness. Never underestimate the power of these gifts. Your heart will begin to hoard these gifts and re-examine them during your deepest moments of grief. They will become healing moments to help you cope with your emotional loss.

Had I not chosen to share my grief with these special people in my life, I would have denied myself their offering of friendship and love for me. The smallest act of kindness can help heal the broken heart and wounded spirit. I discovered that I was gifted with the best friends, gentlest relatives, and most considerate co-workers.

Part 1

They gave me permission to talk—and talk and talk, without being held accountable for what I said or how I felt 15 minutes or an hour or a day ago. Without realizing it, the more I talked and felt their goodness, the more my inner self was beginning to heal. God had truly sent a "network of angels" to watch over me.

Chapter 5

Keeping Busy

After being part of a "twosome" for 26 years, I found it difficult to become accustomed to being alone. After allowing myself some "wallowing" time (my term for laying around feeling sorry for myself), I decided to fill the excess time I had with positive activities. Of course, it was much easier "wallowing", but once I made the conscious decision to move on, I realized it was not constructive or healthy to fill much of the day wasting time. Another step forward for me!

Since I work at a university, we have a two-week winter break in late December and early January. I knew this would be a difficult time for me anyway, because of the holidays, so it was the perfect time to launch my new activity program. I live in a 3-story townhouse with 4 bedrooms, an attic, basement, and garage....plenty of ammunition to begin filling those hours and days. I amazed even myself at how much I accomplished. After loading up the CD player with a stack of favorite music, I started with the basement (which had needed cleaning up for several years). I organized all the tools, camping equipment, craft supplies, games, boxes, and many other items that had been piling up. I sorted, swept, cleaned, dragged, and rearranged everything that did not seem to have a home. That project took me several days. What a sense of accomplishment I had when I stood back and admired the results of my efforts.

Next came the garage. There is a wood stove out there, so I dredged up some old Girl Scout know-how and built a nice fire in the stove. After turning on the radio to the "oldies" station, I backed the car out and set to work on phase 2 of "operation clean-up". I think this day was the first day I sang in months. Once again, I set to work organizing all the clutter, such as contained in most garages. The fire in the wood stove made things cozy, and the music was motivating me....in no time, the place was looking like a model on "This Old

PART 1

House" TV show. After the final touch of sweeping up the floor, I was finished. Again, I amazed myself at my energy and determination. Another project successfully completed.

I took a day or so off to relax and read, drink coffee, and watch "Oprah". I deserved it! The next few days found me tackling the attic. I was getting good at this reorganizing stuff! Boxes were looked through and sorted, clothes tried on, shelves organized....this was even fun! I looked through yearbooks, cards, old letters, and souvenirs. For a while, I forgot what had happened to me in the past months. That was a first! Keeping busy was a great distraction.

Now all the large areas of the house and property were cleaned up. What next? I tackled the closets, one by one. I was a driven woman! One day during a break, I watched a craft show on TV and jotted down the directions to make a wooden radiator enclosure. I had found my next project. My first attempt at carpentry was a success (with a little help from my future son-in-law), and another few days were filled with activity.

As you can see, filling my days with time-consuming projects served two purposes: the obvious—a cleaner, neater house and garage; also, it helped pass many long hours and days giving me more time to constructively heal my wounded self.

Lest you think I intended to work my knuckles to the bone (I must admit I am not a confirmed workaholic), I knew I also deserved some pleasurable activities to fill the time. I liked the positive effect my initiative had evoked. Since that initial burst of energy, I have continued to keep myself busy in order to occupy the hours. I returned to my love of playing the piano, and now play daily. I have also read countless books. Reading is a wonderful way to become lost in another world for a time. I've read everything from novels to suspense to inspirational self-help books. I revived my somewhat meager sewing skills and have made myself several outfits. When spring arrived, I set to work planting seeds indoors and started planning my summer garden early. Countless hours have been spent lost in the rewarding efforts of gardening. I've painted walls and woodwork, rearranged furniture, and made new curtains. The possibilities are endless!

One very important event, which is coming up in the near future, is my daughter, Heather's, wedding. She has inherited my love of "being crafty" (as we call it). We are creating 25 centerpieces for the reception tables and the gift table. I am also using silk flowers to make Heather's bridal bouquet, the bridesmaids' bouquets, and Heather's veil and headpiece. Helping her plan her wedding has become a rewarding activity, and Heather and I are becoming even closer through our many hours spent together.

Even if you've never lifted a hammer or plugged in a glue gun, there are countless activities out there to keep one occupied. I urge you to revive an old hobby, or take a leap into something new (see carpentry project above). One of my most rewarding and constructive projects was to repaint my bedroom and rearrange the furniture. I positioned the bed angled from a corner with a silk tree and light in the corner. It looks striking! I hung lace and flowered curtains and put on a new bedspread. Now it's MY bedroom!

If money is a problem, there are many activities that don't require a monetary investment. Books are available through the public library. Read the "coming events" section of your local newspaper. There are free craft fairs, exhibits, concerts, classes, discussion groups, hiking clubs, and church gatherings, just to name a few.

Perhaps there is a sport you have always wanted to master. Many YWCAs and health clubs offer tennis lessons, aerobics, handball, yoga, dance, swimming, and exercise classes, in addition to many other activities. Physical exercise can be rejuvenating. Now is the time to get out of the house, get those muscles moving, and blood flowing. It may take a bit of courage on your part, but the results can be so rewarding.

Chapter 6

Wake-Up Call

After being married for years, I suppose one falls into comfortable habits. I was unaware that any habits I had acquired warranted the exit my husband took, but I decided eventually to seize the opportunity as a "wake-up call" to perform inventory in myself. (Actually, this was a suggestion from my therapist.)

As I mentioned earlier, I began to lose weight as a result of my initial shock. In reality, this turned out to be a good thing. As most women do (as a result of childbirth and aging), I had gained a little bit of weight each year. But as I now began to drop pounds, I chose to continue to monitor my weight, added aerobic exercise and weight-training, and now weigh 40 pounds less. I feel better physically than I have in 15 years.

I also decided to re-evaluate my mental and emotional attitude. A very good friend (who is also a women's counselor at the YWCA) informed me of a "transitions" seminar which she was preparing to offer. I anxiously agreed to be one of the participants. This decision proved to be one of the most healing events in my life. Eight of us participated in an 8-week series of workshops for personal and spiritual growth. We learned how to encounter ourselves in an entirely new way while enhancing personal growth and individuality. I entered this process in a most enthusiastic frame of mind. We explored our past in order to understand the present and prepare for the future. We were guided in meditations to music, writing exercises, reflections, introspection, sharing, and planning. Our group listened, bonded, and helped each other through a variety of life-stories that had brought us together in this unique series of evenings.

I cannot emphasize strongly enough my enthusiasm for joining a support group. One is able to focus on individual circumstances while becoming enmeshed in the stories and lives of the others in the group. The empathy and encouragement I received from my fellow life-travelers was truly heartwarming and another source of healing for me.

I encourage you to search for such opportunities by attending a seminar, workshop, class, or support group that may become a source of comfort and healing for you, also.

As part of my self-evaluation and improvement, I scheduled an appointment with my doctor for a check-up and to discuss with her my "life change". We talked about my weight loss, nutrition, my weight-training and exercise program. After a check-up and some blood tests, she gave me her approval. I was reassured that I was reacting in a manner that allowed me to be in control of my physical and mental health. My doctor will continue to monitor my health, weight loss, and emotional well being, and has assured me that I am taking all the right steps to adjust to my new life. Another plus for me!

Try to take action that will allow you to feel in control. This is a time when so much that has happened to you is out of your control. There is a feeling of power and satisfaction in knowing that you can and will survive. Even if it is something seemingly small like a new hairdo or a manicure, do it! Begin a home exercise program, or just go outside and take a brisk walk every day. Anything you can do to put yourself in a better frame of mind is a step in the right direction. Healing will occur inch by inch.

Chapter 7

Nature As A Healing Source

Nature has always held an allure for me. I find solace and strength in God's creation. I can say, with all certainty, that I have received unconditional love and comfort from one of God's most loyal creatures—my dog. It may sound odd, but my Labrador retriever, Simon, has been a unique source of love and healing for me. If you are a pet owner, you will identify with my feelings. Simon is my constant companion, always glad to see me when I come home, and a faithful friend always by my side. One day, I was telling my sister what a lifesaver Simon has been in alleviating my loneliness and grief. She said that dogs are a source of perfect, unconditional love…..after all, "dog" is "God" spelled backwards. From that point on, I began to see Simon as another one of my special gifts from God, sent to help me through this trauma.

If you do not have a pet, perhaps you may consider adopting a dog, cat, bunny, bird, hamster, or one of God's other creatures. There are many lonely animals at the Humane League who would like nothing more than to have an owner to shower with love. You are never alone when you are on the receiving end of love from your pet.

Aloneness, which produces silence, can also create opportunities for discovery. As I take walks through the park, I find solace in the songs of the birds, the playfulness of squirrels, and the rustle of a gentle breeze through the treetops. My awareness of nature has been enhanced by the quiet that surrounds me. Many hours have been filled hiking, camping, and enjoying the beauty that the out-of-doors provides. Allow yourself to become aware of the healing that can occur by noticing and appreciating all of God's creation in nature. Listening to the ebb and flow of the ocean or the sound of raindrops can lower blood pressure and create opportunity for meditation. Become lost in observing the calmness of fluffy clouds floating through a vibrant blue sky. Notice a butterfly gliding quietly by, a lightning bug twinkling in the evening dusk, or a bee gathering nectar from a flower. You have the time to savor the lovely moments nature has to offer. Accept each moment as the tiny gift it truly can be.

I recently spent a 3-day weekend at a cabin in a state park in Pennsylvania with three girlfriends. We enjoyed the simplicity of camping meals, long walks, a roaring campfire under a brilliantly starry sky, and the slower pace that comes with being in the woods. The beauty of waterfalls, ferns, wildflowers, moss, and wildlife encountered during our hikes comforted us. The warm sun and gentle breeze refreshed us as we sat by the edge of a lovely lake. The cool protection of giant pine trees gave us reason to pause and reflect on the awesome strength in nature. I was rejuvenated that weekend, and I draw on my memories to continue to replenish my need for nature as a healer.

If you have the opportunity, allow yourself to relish whatever bit of God's natural creation is available to you. I hope you will discover the savoring of nature as a powerful source of comfort.

Chapter 8
Keeping A Journal

One of the first suggestions my therapist, Susanne, gave me when I began counseling sessions with her was to consider keeping a journal. Writing my feelings became a source of escape for me. This was especially true in the first days and weeks of my crisis when I had not told anyone about my husband's admission of betrayal. I felt so alone. My journal became my friend…I could say anything that was on my mind, and believe me, I did! I poured my heart out on those pages.

I began my journal writing as a release for my feelings of intense disbelief and abandonment. As time went by, these emotions were replaced by numbness, and eventually anger. I believe I was experiencing the same type of feelings one encounters after the death of a loved one. However, in this situation, it was an emotional death rather than a physical one. Although I appeared calm on the outside, inside I was becoming a vessel of turmoil. My therapist began to see the change in me and urged me to start to unleash those feelings. She became the sounding board for the release of my anger and also suggested physical exercise as another way to vent.

Most days after I came home from work, I put my dog on his leash and stomped out into the evening, my legs pumping as quickly as my mind was churning. I had confrontations with my husband in my mind and called him every name in the book. Then I confronted "the other woman" and let her have a piece of my mind. Sometimes I walked long after dark, venting until I was drained!! Then I'd come home and write it all down in my journal. My anger needed to come out…..it was being purged. My closest friends and family members also encouraged me to free myself by allowing me to share those dark feelings with them. As time went by, my anger began to subside. I was having my say, even if sometimes it was only to myself.

I could feel the healing results of releasing my feelings, especially writing them down on paper in my journal.

My journal is filled with many chapters, and as time elapsed, I continued to record my feelings of confusion, pain, and whatever emotions unfolded as long as I needed to do so. Keeping that negativity bottled up inside myself would be self-destructive. As long as I release it in a constructive way, I am healing.

Occasionally I would re-read those pages overflowing with grief and confusion, and realize that I truly have come a long way. Once again, I attribute my progress to God's influence in my life. "God helps those who help themselves", and He gave me the strength to take each tiny step to climb up out of that dark and scary hole I had been pushed into by Ed's betrayal.

My therapist, Susanne, gave me another suggestion that I found to be very healing. She encouraged me to write a letter to "the other woman". She said whether I mailed it to her or not, I might find it good therapy to pour out my feelings to this person who played a major part in turning my life upside down. I DID write that letter, and I chose NOT to mail it. But Susanne was correct in her prediction that simply writing it would provide another outlet for my hurt. It helped me to purge those feelings by putting them into words on paper.

The transitions workshop sessions provided many opportunities to use writing as therapy. As we were given topics for thought and led through guided meditations and readings, my mind produced recollections which I was able to express on paper. This was a satisfying accomplishment, and I treasure the words I composed from my personal journey through introspection. Writing in your own diary or journal can be immensely freeing. I wrote simply to release the thoughts racing in my head. Once I started writing, the words tumbled onto the paper, filling page after page.

One of the guided meditations presented to us during the workshop took place while listening to quiet, instrumental music and the ocean tide. We were instructed to envision a peaceful beach scene that would become a time of healing for ourselves, and then

Part 1

to write about it in detail. Following are the words I wrote after this particular meditation:

"The sand was soft and warm. I was close to the water's edge and watched the ebb and flow of the gentle tide. This was a scene from my past when my daughter, Heather, and I lay on a blanket on the beach together, enjoying the oneness of contentment and nature. I saw a seagull land very near to me. He had only one leg and a partial stump. The wind kept blowing him as he stood on his one leg, and every so often, he would lightly touch his stub to the ground to steady himself. He kept his eyes closed, and he, too, was enjoying the warmth and the quiet. I was touched by his acceptance of his handicap—it did not cause him to cease enjoying his moments in the sun. He gave me the gift of acceptance, and believing in myself to continue on with my life."

I quickly realized that I enjoyed writing, not only descriptive bits and pieces of imagery such as the seagull story, but also about my real-life emotions and situation. My workshop companions encouraged me by their reactions to my writing, and it is partially due to their encouragement that I am writing this book. I realized that I could not change what Ed had done to our marriage, to my life. I was determined not to become a bitter person as a result of my pain. To be thrown off the path of life that was familiar to me, and wounded so severely by the roadblock in my way, could have caused me to give up. For a brief time, I may have even considered that route. My writing gave me the opportunity to "tap into my creative spirit", and I discovered the power I have within myself. Writing has been a significant tool for my empowerment.

If you choose to keep a diary or journal, no one need ever read what you write. Your written words can become a coping mechanism, preserved for you to re-read, if you so desire. Some find it healing to write their deepest thoughts and later burn the pages as a symbolic expression of obstacles overcome. This method can serve as a tool to "let go" of overwhelming anger and frustration.

Chapter 9

Warning Signs

I thought Edward and I had one of those marriages that was meant to be. Throughout our years together, many of our friends often remarked that we still behaved like newlyweds. I considered us to be best friends, soul mates, lovers….our hearts were connected. I have no doubt in my mind that our marriage was one of the best ever. How, then, did this "storybook" marriage result in causing so much pain and heartache? This question has haunted me, and it is only in retrospect that I have begun to recognize the small, subtle signs of the erosion of our marital closeness that might have served as warning signs to me. Up until the very end (perhaps the last year or so), I had no reason to question any of Ed's actions. He was my husband, my partner, the one who made me feel like a loved wife….I trusted him explicitly. And that is the precise reason why I did not realize that something might be wrong in our marriage.

My husband's infidelity actually began at least a year prior to his telling me he was leaving. He left me for a co-worker with whom he spent every working day, side by side, for seven years. I suppose I should feel some pride in knowing that it took that long to wear him down. This "friend" sat with us at company holiday parties, summer picnics, and at many after-work gatherings. I was aware of her admiration for my husband, but my trust in him kept me from being suspicious of their relationship.

In our last year together, I recognized an ever-so-slightly nagging feeling within myself—that things seemed a bit "different" between Ed and me. For many years, he called me each day on his break at work. That brief phone call was a bright spot in both of our days. However, his calls began to dwindle, then stopped altogether. When I mentioned how much I missed his phone calls, he explained that he was just too busy at work to take breaks any more. I sympathized with him that he was working so hard.

Part 1

Soon he began napping often (when he came home from work each afternoon, and again after dinner each evening). Soon these "naps" became deep sleeps that lasted the entire evening. I usually had to awaken him to come to bed at night. (Again, there was the excuse that he was exhausted from work.) He was increasingly too tired for conversation or other activities we could do together. In retrospect, I realize that sleep was his escape from me.

For many years, Ed had gone fishing or hunting one evening per week and a few hours each weekend. These expeditions became much more frequent, often as many as two or three weeknights and an entire Saturday or Sunday. Sometimes he even returned home after dark because he said he had found a great fishing spot in the next county. Although I did question him, there was always a logical explanation.

You may wonder why I did not become more suspicious, due to these warning signs. My intuition did tell me that something was "not quite right", but I always dismissed it thinking, "Maybe this is just how marriage is after 26 years." I did suggest that we attend a "marriage weekend" being offered through our church, but Ed was pretty adamant about not wanting to attend. Now I know why. I will always wonder if I should have relied on that intuitive feeling and pursued the matter further. I will never know.

My reason for mentioning these incidents is that sometimes we need to rely on that little voice in our heads called "intuition". If habits change, explanations seem weak, and things just don't seem quite right, trust that gut feeling. Ask questions, seek answers, and search out the truth. If that nagging feeling won't go away, suggest that the two of you seek counseling to iron out the rough spots. Make any suggestion that you think will help you to get to the bottom of what may or may not be a problem. It is better to be safe than sorry. Perhaps if I had been more insistent, Ed and I could have begun to repair the damage to our marriage before it was too late. I now know that if this could happen to us in our "storybook" marriage, it could happen to anyone.

Chapter 10
Make a Plan for the Future

It has taken determination to be able to admit to myself that my life will go on... but not in the way that I had imagined. I am learning to be strong and to instill in myself the will to step into the future with a plan. I will not continue to be a victim. I will take charge of my emotions and my life.

As an important part of the support group sessions I attended, one of the exercises we performed was to choose ten values that held particular worthiness for us at this time in our lives. We were to list these values, place them in order of priority, and write a sentence or two about each. I found this to be an important beginning to my self-awareness, and this exercise caused me to admit much to myself. Perhaps such an activity would benefit others in recognizing the goodness that exists in each of us. I would like to share the list of my values with you. They represent my innermost feelings during this journey. Perhaps you may identify with some of these:

1. Uniqueness: I am aware that each person is unique...I want to nurture my own uniqueness, make it obvious to myself, and to foster it in others.

2. Aliveness/Spirit: I long to feel alive again...I have felt nearly dead, and I ache to feel truly alive, filled with spirit and passion for living each day.

3. Sense of Humor: For so long, I could not laugh; but as I heal, I regain my sense of humor. It was dormant but is re-emerging, and that gives me hope in myself.

4. Genuineness: I cannot bear fakes or frauds. I pray for the ability to exhibit myself as I truly am... to wear my "self" proudly and stand strong and firm in my morals and beliefs.

Part 1

5. *Tenderness:* A tender, gentle soul dwells within me, and it is a most important part of my strength. The inner "me" is one of gentleness.

6. *Perseverance:* There is a feeling of lasting accomplishment in perseverance, and I hope that I have the strength to persevere and discover what life has in store for me.

7. *Compassion:* My compassion for others, both human and animal, is both a blessing and a curse, but I would rather suffer for and with others than deny myself the ability to feel with love.

8. *Playfulness:* I am an imp at heart. May I never lose the playfulness that makes life fun. What would my life be without it?

9. *Simplicity:* Let me not become entangled in "things". Life's simple joys are the ones that I hold dearest in my heart... family, friends, faith, nature, love – untouchable but more valuable than words can tell.

10. *Awareness of self:* I want to truly know myself - not to hide from any part of the real "me". Even if it is painful, I want to learn from what I am living through and go on with my life, better for what I have endured.

    Re-reading my values affirms my belief in myself. Although I could have allowed my husband's betrayal to continue to darken my life, but instead I have chosen to create positive energy from a negative situation. Permit yourself the opportunity to recognize the goodness within you. This step is a positive, self-affirming accomplishment.

Each of us possesses valuable God-given traits.
Use the choices on the following list to inspire you
to recognize the goodness from God within yourself!!

Accepting
Active
Affectionate
Ambitious
Appreciative
Attentive
Bold
Brave
Careful
Caring
Cautious
Clear thinking
Committed
Compassionate
Concerned
Confident
Considerate
Consistent
Content
Courageous
Creative
Decisive
Dedicated
Dependable
Determined
Devoted
Disciplined
Effective
Empathetic
Encouraging
Energetic
Ethical
Faithful
Fervent
Forgiving
Funny
Gentle
Genuine
Generous
Gracious

Grateful
Hard working
Helpful
Honorable
Hopeful
Humble
Humorous
Impulsive
Independent
Influential
Innocent
Joyful
Just
Kind
Leader
Lively
Loving
Loyal
Merciful
Moral
Motivated
Obedient
Open-minded
Optimistic
Organized
Patient
Peaceful
Perseverant
Persistent
Playful
Pleasant
Practical
Prayerful
Productive
Protective
Pure
Quiet
Resourceful
Respectful
Responsible

Responsive
Restful
Reverent
Righteous
Romantic
Self-controlled
Sensitive
Simple
Spirit-filled
Spiritual
Strong
Submissive
Successful
Sympathetic
Tender
Thoughtful
Trusting
Trustworthy
Truthful
Understanding
Unique
Unselfish
Warm
Willing
Wise
Witty
Worthy

Part 1

On the last evening in my series of transitions workshops, we were instructed to write our "plan for the future". We had spent several weeks preparing ourselves for this daunting task. We had learned how to achieve greater intimacy with our "inner selves", and now it was time to respond to our life situation in a creative way. Again, we began our exercise with calming music and introspection. As I began to write, my future plans seemed to flow from within my soul. I am certain that each of us holds hopes and dreams within ourselves. They need not be magnificent or earth-shattering (mine certainly are not). They merely need to be sincere responses to our inner longings. The following are the "life plans" that I have written for myself:

1. To whole-heartedly explore in every way, and to bravely exhaust all means to determine my true feelings about Edward's betrayal before I come to closure; to be brave enough to accept what will be known in my heart and in my head.

2. To allow myself time to heal, to create something positive from my pain, and to try to retain my trusting nature, even though it has been damaged by betrayal.

3. To pray each day; to remember how important God is in my life, and to always know that I am special to Him. He holds me in the palm of His hand.

4. To not gain back the weight I have lost. I feel pretty again; for the first time in years, I like the way I look.

5. To remember that my children are not little kids anymore who need my comments on everything. To not offer unasked-for advice...listen and accept!

6. To exercise in some way every day—by walking, weight-training, aerobics, bicycling. I feel alive when I am physically fit!

7. *To learn new music on the piano; not to be content to play the same songs... challenge, practice, and learn!*

8. *To be of service to others—to help in any and all small ways that I am able. Every act of kindness benefits both the receiver and the giver.*

9. *To take care of my health—my body, mind, and spirit—by proper nourishment.*

10. *To travel—the outdoors calls to me. I long to experience the beauty of the Grand Canyon, the Rocky Mountains, the clean fresh air of a country I have not yet experienced.*

All of my goals are simple, practical, and feasible. I did not make any choices in this "plan for my future" that are not possible. In doing so, I have assured myself that I will attain them. Believe in yourself and in what you want to achieve. In the stillness of your expectant heart, let your goodness arise.

EPILOGUE TO PART 1

The previous chapters have chronicled my journey through the shock, denial, fear, and finally recognition of betrayal. Life will go on. I am surviving. In the beginning of my journey, I fought valiantly to face the mind-numbing truth. I struggled so painfully to simply exist through each minute, hour, and day. As time progressed, I stepped gingerly along the way, accepting the reality of my circumstances. Now I look to the future with increasing strength, self-confidence, and fortitude.

Believe me, this has not been an easy journey. I have had to reach down within myself and summon up every ounce of courage within my being. I am living proof that the human spirit can survive overwhelming sadness. My faith, family, friends, and my own strength have lifted me up, carried me along, and sent me on my way. I do not know what life holds for me. But I do know that I will be able to look any obstacle in the face and not allow it to have the last word. Equally significant, I am learning to forgive. This most difficult feat has helped to move me out of anger and toward the quiet strength and inner peace I have been seeking. I have come to realize that this, too, shall pass. I AM SURVIVING!!!

PART 2
SPIRITUAL HEALING

Chapter 11
Who God Is

For many of you, Faith in God will be a very confusing thing. Many Christians have been taught that God is often the one who sends the pain into your life. Or, that He "allows" the pain, even though He may not have been the author of it. If this describes you, please know that you are not alone. Although this is a very common teaching among Christians, it is a teaching that will immediately short circuit any progress you might make toward survival, healing, and victory.

Therefore, it is imperative that we understand who God really is—that is, who the Bible reveals Him to be in actual fact, all traditional teaching aside. I want to invest some time into looking, without pre-conceived notions, at simply what the Scripture says about this subject. Once we have done this, I am confident that you will be able to trust Him. Without this trust, victory cannot be realized.

First, let's dispense with some common misconceptions about who God is. He is not Santa Claus, gleefully granting every wish and prayer that we utter. Neither is He the "Divine Bully", sitting in heaven holding a large fly swatter, carefully watching our every move and swatting us immediately whenever we step out of line. He is not a tyrant who demands unending perfection; He is not detached from our lives, sitting in heaven simply observing from a distance; and He is not dead. Lastly, He is not an arbitrary person, sometimes doing good, and sometimes not—but you can never be sure.

The real God is revealed for us in the Scriptures. The following is a partial list of Scriptures which define Him:

1. James 1:17 says "Every good gift and every perfect gift is from above and cometh down from the Father of Lights..." That is, God is good, and He's good all the time. (Yes, bad things do happen. Later in the chapter, you will find a list of characteristics that will pinpoint the source of our difficulties.)

PART 2

2. Psalm 118:6 says "The Lord is on my side." If He is on my side, how can He be against me at the same time? If He is on my side, how can He be the One who brings trial and trouble into my life? The answer is, He cannot.

3. Proverbs 18:10 says "The name of the Lord is a strong tower: the righteous run into it, and are safe." The Lord, therefore, is our Protector. He is the one who keeps us from harm, not the one who brings harm to us.

4. James 1:13 says "...for God cannot be tempted with evil, neither tempteth He any man." The word "tempted" here can also be translated as trial or problem. This verse, which is God's Word, says that God never sends trials or problems into our life.

5. 1 Corinthians 10:13 says "There hath no temptation taken you but such as is common to man: but God is faithful, who will not suffer you to be tempted above that ye are able; but will with the temptation also make a way to escape, that ye may be able to bear it." This Scripture is regularly misinterpreted to read that God is the one sending the temptation or the trial. Notice, however, that the verse does not say that. It says that any trial that has overtaken you is "common to man", meaning that it is something that other humans have experienced. God is the One who limits the trial or temptation, and also the One who provides the way to escape it. (That "way" is Faith in the written promises of the New Testament.)

6. John 1:14 says that Jesus Christ is "full of grace and truth". He is full of grace, which means that He looks upon us with favor, no matter what. If He is full of grace, there is no room for anything else. The same logic applies to truth.

7. 1 John 4:8 says "God is love." Notice that it does not say merely that God shows love, or that God feels love, but that God IS love. God, therefore, is pure love. How could a God who is pure love do or allow anything to bring pain into the life of someone He loves?

8. John 1:4 says that "God is light". Since this is true, He can have no part in darkness, or anything related to it.

9. John 1:3 and John 10:10 both indicate that "God is life". The Scripture in John 10 says that He gives life, and that more abundantly. Once again, we see God separated from anything connected with death or sin, neither of which can have anything to do with spiritual life.

10. John 8:32 says "And ye shall know the truth, and the truth shall make you free." Verse 36 in the same chapter says "If the Son therefore make you free, ye shall be free indeed." The Lord is about freedom. He is the One who sets you free, not the one who places you in difficult circumstances, which are related to bondage.

11. II Peter 1:4 says that God is the giver of an incorruptible inheritance reserved in heaven for you. Coupled with the fact that God is love, we see that, once again, He is described as a giver (not a taker). He gives sacrificially, and He gives all that He has because He loves us.

12. Hebrews 7:25 says that "...He ever liveth to make intercession for us". As our Intercessor, He is the One who defends us, who speaks out on our behalf when our enemy, the devil, makes accusation against us. Notice that Jesus ever lives to do this, which means that He has no time left to accuse us or cause us harm.

13. I John 2:1 says "If any man sin, we have an Advocate with the Father, Jesus Christ, the Righteous." The closest thing we have in our society to an advocate would be a defense lawyer. An advocate is one who encourages us, supports us, strengthens us, defends us, and is always FOR us, never against us.

14. Psalm 23:1 says "The Lord is my Shepherd..." As my Shepherd, He watches over me, and protects me from all harm. He sees to it that I am properly nourished, and that I am happy and content. A reading of Psalm 23 in its entirety will give

a vivid picture of this care. Not one item in the Psalm even hints at anything but love, care, and positive reinforcement.

15. Genesis 22:14 calls Him "Jehovah-Jireh". This Hebrew name can be translated "The Lord my Provider". As He did for Abraham and Isaac in Genesis 22, the Lord always provides our needs.

He gave His own life for you and me. Scripture says that there is no greater love than this, but that a man lay down his life for another. God sent His only begotten Son to live, and then give His life on this earth to pay sin's penalty for human beings who could never pay this penalty themselves. We know it as the Crucifixion, or Calvary. It is, by far, the greatest act of love of all time.

God is good, all the time. Although only a few of His attributes are listed, Scripture is consistent in presenting a God who is only positive toward His children.

We must keep in mind that God works through faith in His Word. It is only through faith—our faith—that we will experience His goodness and love.

How, then, do we account for the fact that we experience pain, disappointment, sickness, discouragement, betrayal, and a host of other evils in our earthly life? Let's take a look at some more Scripture, but this time, we will list the Biblical characteristics of our enemy, the devil. Ironically, it is by looking at him that we begin to see the truth of his character, and the common mistake of attributing these characteristics to God. Some of the devil's traits are:

1. John 10:10 says that the devil is a thief, and is come "to steal, kill and destroy". These are three of his main characteristics. Anything that involves stealing, killing or destroying of anything in your life can be attributed to the devil.

2. John 8:44 says that the devil is a liar. More than that, it says that he is the father of all liars. That is, everything that comes out of his mouth is a lie. He, then, would be the one who would

be telling human beings that his own characteristics belong to God. Each time, it is a lie.

3. Genesis 3:1 tells us that the first time the devil opens his mouth, he does so to place doubt on the Word of God. Since this is the first time the devil speaks in the Bible, and the first time he appears in the Bible, according to what is known as the Law of First Mention (a principle of Bible interpretation), this trait will also be a prominent one for the devil. His mission is to convince human beings, not that the Word of God is purely false, but that it "just might not be true in your case". Satan's idea is to place just the slightest doubt into your mind, which is sufficient to keep you from exercising faith in the Word of God.

4. Genesis 3 is the story of satan's temptation of Eve and then Adam, in the Garden of Eden. It is the devil, then, who is the author of temptation (trial, problems, difficulties).

5. Revelation 12:9 says that the devil is a deceiver. His goal is to trick you, or charm you, or somehow convince you that his way is right, and the Bible way is wrong. Deceit is an especially evil quality, in that the deceiver often appears as a friend or someone you can trust.

6. Revelation 12:10 calls the devil "the accuser of the brethren". Every day, he invests his time in accusing each Christian of wrongdoing before God the Father. How wonderful that one of the characteristics of Jesus Christ is that He is our Advocate.

7. I Peter 5:8 calls the devil "our adversary". Just as we saw that God is for us, the devil is against us. He stands against us in every way possible, but, since he is also a deceiver, it is sometimes difficult (unless you know who God is) to determine that he is standing against you.

8. I Corinthians 14:33 tells us that "God is not the author of confusion". If God is not the author of it, then the devil must be.

PART 2

9. Isaiah 14:12-15 describes satan's heavenly rebellion when he was known as Lucifer. It catalogs a blatant stand against the Creator. Ever since then, rebellion has been characteristic of the devil and his followers.

10. Isaiah 14:12-15 also displays what may be satan's primary trait, which is pride. His position in Heaven as Lucifer was that of "the anointed cherub that covered the throne". He was one of the most important beings in all of heaven, but it wasn't enough for him. Pride drove him to oppose his very Maker.

11. Genesis 3:1 also tells us that, as the serpent, the devil was "subtle". This is a word that means "tricky" or "sneaky". These characteristics work hand in hand with deceit and lying. What it tells us is that the devil's workings in our lives will not be obvious to us. In fact, we will not be aware of them without at least some knowledge of Scripture, and the leading of the Holy Spirit (both of which are easily available to any Christian).

12. Hebrews 2:15 tells us that the devil is connected with two other attributes—death and bondage. It should be no surprise that he is connected with death, which is the opposite of life. But it should be instructive that he is connected with bondage. Anything—repeat anything—that keeps you in bondage is a clear indication of the work of our enemy.

13. Other items that are connected with the devil include: darkness, hate, counterfeit (especially in spiritual things), hurt, pain, disappointment, discouragement, anger, revenge, jealousy, attack, control, mocking, betrayal, and anything overly rigid or strict.

The spiritual atmosphere that allows the devil's characteristics to flourish is FEAR. Just as nothing can be done for good in the spiritual realm without faith in God's Word, nothing can be done in this life that is destructive, painful and harmful without fear, which is, in reality, simply faith in the devil's words.

Notice that almost all of the devil's characteristics are the exact opposite of God's attributes. Notice, too, that you now have many of these characteristics listed on paper. Did you notice how many of satan's characteristics are often blamed on God—most often, by those who are God's own children? Perhaps we are victims of the deceit that is characteristic of our enemy far more often than we might have thought.

Now, however, you have been provided with a tool that can be of great help to you in your daily experiences. Whenever a situation arises, simply look at its characteristics, find it on one of the above lists, and you will know where it comes from. In doing so, over time you will come to appreciate God's true nature, and the many, many times He has been falsely accused of things the devil has done. When we first realized this, we were overwhelmed with a sense of regret, but also with a deep appreciation of His patience and grace. God IS good, and is willing to endure this pain—His love for us is that big.

Chapter 12

Who You Are In Christ

One of the biggest problems you face in this matter of relationship betrayal is that of your self-esteem—it has been absolutely crushed. In my case, I said to myself, "Someone who spent years and years with me, and who knows me as well as anyone else on earth, considers me to be a THROWAWAY. They have made the choice to be unwilling to spend any time with me. They want only to be someplace else." It isn't very flattering!! In fact, it is a major torpedo to your feelings of worth. Because this event is the most prominent thing in your life at the time, your tendency will be to let this event determine your future. Far too many people make this choice.

There are a number of different ways that self-worth can be determined. Among these are:
 a) What others think of you
 b) What you think of yourself
 c) What family, friends, or enemies say
 d) What your former relationship partner said and did

Most people assess their worth using one or more of these items. But, there is another way to determine your worth, and that is to consider what God says about you.

It cannot be overemphasized that this issue is foundational to your healing. If this issue is not properly addressed, your healing will be short-circuited, and you will never realize the future that the Lord wants you to have. So, let's look at what God says about who you are. Afterward, you will have to choose what you will believe about yourself. Will you believe what God says, or what other people say? Will you believe what God says, or what you think about yourself? Will you believe God, or your former relationship partner?

The following Scriptures tell us who we are in Christ from God's point of view. Each Scripture is taken directly from the Bible, without private interpretation, and without embellishment of any kind. In God's eyes, you are:

1) Light of the world - Matthew 5:14 "Ye are the light of the world." That is, YOU are the light; He shines through you.

2) A child of God - John 1:12 "But as many as received Him, to them gave He power to become the sons of God." At salvation, you become God's child. While it is true that you are an adopted child (Romans 8), you have every legal standing as His child.

3) Part of the true vine - John 15:5 "I am the vine, ye are the branches." Jesus is the vine, and we are the branches. But, because we are connected directly to Him, we are everything that He is.

4) A friend of God - John 15:15 "Henceforth I call you not servants; ... but I have called you friends." God considers you to be not just His child, not just His willing servant, not just some human being, but HIS PERSONAL FRIEND.

5) Joint heir - Romans 8:17 "And if children, then heirs; heirs of God, and joint-heirs with Christ." The wording here is important. Notice that we are called "joint heirs". On this earth, when we inherit anything, we do so as a co-heir. That is, the inheritance is divided among several people, and we get just a part. To be a joint heir means that the entire inheritance belongs to us.

6) His temple - I Corinthians 6:19 "Your body is the temple of the Holy Ghost which is in you, which ye have of God, and ye are not your own." Just as the Old Testament Tabernacle, and later the Temple were buildings in which God dwelt, we ourselves—our human bodies—have become His dwelling place under New Testament Christianity. The Old Testament buildings were of the finest workmanship; the best materials;

and the most beautiful of all the buildings of the earth. The Lord says that WE have become just like that in His sight.

7) His body - I Corinthians 12:27 "Now ye are the body of Christ." He is the Head; and we are the Body. He is in heaven at this time; so we are His Body in visible form on the earth.

8) A new creature—made new - II Corinthians 5:17 "If any man be in Christ, he is a new creature: old things are passed away; behold, all things are become new." While your reflection in the mirror may look the same to you, your spiritual self has been totally renewed. You have become a creature of unspeakable beauty and power. God's Word says so.

9) Part of His family - Galatians 3:26-28 "For ye are all the children of God by faith in Christ Jesus. ... There is neither Jew nor Greek, ... there is neither male nor female: for ye are all one in Christ Jesus." We have been given the privilege of becoming just as much a part of God's family as Abraham himself. Every promise given to Abraham, David, and any other member of our family is given to us.

10) Heirs of every promise - Galatians 3:29 (NLT) "Now that you belong to Christ, you are the true children of Abraham. You are his heirs, and now all the promises God gave to him belong to you." Please notice: we are heirs of EVERY PROMISE. The New Testament contains many hundreds of promises. Every single one applies to you and me with the same force that it applies to Jesus Himself.

11) Redeemed - Galatians 3:13 "Christ hath redeemed us." To be redeemed means "to be bought back from". We were bought back from the clutches of sin and the devil by the shed blood of Jesus Christ. He gave His life, paid for our sin, and then gave that payment to us for free. "No one ever cared for me like Jesus."

12) A saint - Ephesians 1:1 "... to the saints which are at Ephesus, and to the faithful in Christ Jesus"; Phil 1:1 "... to all the saints in Christ Jesus which are at Philippi." I am aware of

the common teaching that saints were special human beings who did great deeds, and who receive special recognition in heaven. The Word of God teaches, on the other hand, that every person who receives Jesus Christ as their personal Savior becomes a saint. Being called a saint has nothing to do with your life or accomplishments, and everything to do with His.

13) God's workmanship - Ephesians 2:10 "For we are His workmanship, created in Christ Jesus." How can God's workmanship be defective, or stained, or weak, or broken? When God makes things, He makes them whole, right, and without flaw.

14) Righteous - II Corinthians 5:21 "For He hath made Him to be sin for us, who knew no sin; that we might be made the righteousness of God in Him." Notice that this verse tells us that we have become the righteousness of God. It does not say that our conduct is perfect. Rather, it indicates that we have been given another free gift—the righteousness of Jesus Christ to claim as our own.

15) Seated in heavenly places - Ephesians 2:6 "And hath raised us up together, and made us sit together in heavenly places in Christ Jesus." Yes, I know that you are present on the earth. Nevertheless, the Bible says that we are seated in heavenly places with Jesus, and it says this in the present tense. Once again, the Bible is speaking of the spiritual reality as the primary fact rather than the physical reality (which is only temporary).

16) Living by the law of the Spirit of Life - Romans 8:2 "For the law of the Spirit of life in Christ Jesus hath made me free from the law of sin and death." Prior to our salvation, we lived by the "law of sin and death". That is the law of the world, and the law that the devil seeks to keep us bound to after we know Jesus as Savior. But we are not bound to that law any longer. We now live by the law of the Spirit of LIFE in Christ Jesus. Ours is an emphasis on life, not death; on victory, not defeat; on the positive, not the negative.

17) Free from bondage to anything - John 8:32,36 "And ye shall know the truth, and the truth shall make you free. ... If the Son therefore shall make you free, ye shall be free indeed." Isn't this Scripture a blessing? Doesn't it put a big smile on your face to know that you are free from any bondage? No earthly thing, and no lie of the devil, can ever keep you captive—ever again.

18) Have the mind of Christ - I Corinthians 2:16 "... But we have the mind of Christ." My human mind has a failing memory. I have to write notes to myself sometimes. But the Word of God says that I have the mind of Christ. It is a good mind; a mind that's sharp; the best mind one can have. God says so.

19) Can do what He did on earth - John 14:12 "Verily, verily, I say unto you, he that believeth on Me, the works that I do shall he do also; and greater works than these shall he do; because I go unto My Father." This is one of the most startling Scriptures that I know. Yet, it is spoken by Jesus Christ Himself, and it is spoken to human beings—believers—just like you and me. The verse begins with the phrase, "Verily, verily", which is used by the Lord to call special attention to this utterance. He knew that our human minds would have trouble believing this, but He said it anyway, because it is true.

20) Royalty....the child of a King - I John 3:2 "Beloved, now are we the sons of God." I was taught that, though I was saved, I was still a "lowly worm, not worthy to even raise my eyes toward Jesus". It was a sincere teaching, but it kept me in bondage for many years. The Bible says that I am the child of a King; a child of God Himself; part of the family of God; part of Christ's own body. That would make me a prince, a member of the royal family. My Father is a King—THE KING.

21) A priest of God - I Peter 2:9 "But ye are a chosen generation, a royal priesthood." You are chosen, upon salvation, to serve in a priestly capacity in a way similar to that of the priests in the Old Testament. That is, you are to intercede on behalf of others to God. In the Old Testament, the priest did so by

offering animal sacrifices and doing the work of the tabernacle or temple. For us, this priestly work involves prayer. It is our calling—our ministry—our privilege to be allowed to intercede in prayer for each other, for those who don't know God, and for those who are away from Him.

22) Have Jesus dwelling within you - I John 4:4 "Greater is He that is in you, than he that is in the world." Jesus Christ, who defeated sin, hell, the grave, death, and the devil, resides inside you and me. Jesus is the power of the universe and has proven it through the Resurrection. By dwelling inside you, His power and authority become yours.

23) An overcomer through faith - I John 5:4 "For whatsoever is born of God overcometh the world: and this is the victory that overcometh the world, even our faith." The overcoming mentioned in this verse is accomplished only by the joining of His power with your faith. If either ingredient is missing, there is no overcoming. However, if you will exercise faith in His power, He says that you have already overcome, because He has already overcome.

24) You have faith - Romans 12:3 "... God hath dealt to every man the measure of faith." I often hear people say that they have no faith, or pray that their faith be increased. But this verse says that all people who know Jesus have been given "THE measure of faith". Therefore, you do have faith, and it is all the faith you need because Jesus says so in His Word. It is evident that this faith can be measured and, in it's briefest form, the measure of your faith is the amount of the Word of God that you have within you. Therefore, to an extent, the measure of the strength of your faith is dependent upon your willingness to increase the amount and strength of it.

25) Exactly like Jesus....on this earth - I John 4:17 "Herein is our love made perfect, that we may have boldness in the day of judgment: because as He is, so are we in this world." To me, this is one of the most startling, and yet one of the most important verses in the Bible. If you look at it carefully, it tells us that we as saved Christians are (present tense) "as He is"

(that is, exactly like Jesus is now). That is an overwhelmingly powerful statement, and I know it runs contrary to traditional Christian teaching. However, that is exactly what this verse says. Better yet, it adds that we are exactly like Him "in this world". So, it is not something we look forward to when we get to heaven, but it is our condition right now, right here in our life on earth.

26) Given His authority over the devil - James 4:7 "Submit yourselves therefore to God. Resist the devil, and he will flee from you." I know that the devil and his helpers are spiritual beings, and they have been around for a long time. They are experienced, nasty, and ever-vigilant. Yet, the Scriptures clearly tell us that Jesus defeated them totally at His crucifixion and resurrection. Just as He gave His salvation to us, just as He gave His righteousness to us, He also gave His authority over the forces of darkness to His children. This verse plainly says, "Resist the devil, and he will flee from YOU." So, praying to Jesus to have Him chase the devil from our lives is a prayer that cannot be answered unless He would violate His own Word. He instructs US to resist the devil—in His Name, because He supplies the power—and the devil will flee from us. We have a vital part to play, as we are to speak against the devil in Jesus' Name. If we do, he has to flee, and he does.

27) Possessor of abundant life - John 10:10 "I am come that they might have life, and that they might have it more abundantly." Abundant life includes eternal life, but does not end there. Abundant life is given to us for this life on earth, and includes the authority over the forces of darkness that we mentioned in #26. It includes physical health and healing, prosperity, protection, and fruitfulness. All of these were given to us freely at the moment we received Jesus as our Savior.

28) Can do all things through Christ - Phil 4:13 "I can do all things through Christ which strengtheneth me." If we will believe this verse, we must eliminate the phrase "I can't" from our vocabulary. The God whom we serve is someone to whom nothing is impossible. If we are in Him, and He is in us, there is nothing that can't be accomplished.

29) Safe from weapons formed against you - Isaiah 54:17 "No weapon that is formed against thee shall prosper; ... This is the heritage of the servants of the LORD." This is one of our favorite verses in the Bible. It is a flat statement with no exceptions, telling us that no weapon—physical or spiritual, wielded by anyone, any time, or any place—can prosper against us. It doesn't mean we won't be attacked, but it does mean that the attack need not succeed if we apply the other aspects of our life in Christ that are in this list. What a tremendous comfort and blessing this verse is.

30) Totally forgiven - Colossians 2:13 "And you, being dead in your sins ..., hath He quickened together with Him, having forgiven you all trespasses." I know that sometimes we don't feel forgiven, and that sometimes we don't believe we deserve to be forgiven. But this verse unmistakably states that Jesus paid for all trespasses—past, present, and future—when He died on the cross. He forgave you at Calvary. This is not, of course, an invitation to go out and sin (which one who truly loves Him would not do), but a reminder that it is always right to forgive oneself.

31) Free from fear - II Timothy 1:7 "For God hath not given us the spirit of fear; but of power, and of love, and of a sound mind." Fear, as we will see in a later chapter, is the opposite of faith and one of our biggest enemies in this life on earth. Please notice that this verse plainly tells us that fear is a "spirit". The world teaches that fear is an emotion, and is a normal part of life. The Bible says fear is a spirit, and therefore a spiritual being which imposes itself upon you UNLESS you resist it as described in #26.

32) On God's side - Romans 8:31 "What shall we then say to these things? If God be for us, who can be against us?" He is FOR you, not against you. He is on your side. He is never against you. He wants you to succeed. He is looking for ways to bless you. He wants only the best for you, and never—NEVER—seeks to do you harm.

33) More than a conqueror - Romans 8:37 "In all these things we are more than conquerors through Him that loved us." It would be enough to be a conqueror, but He says you are more than a conqueror. I believe that means that we not only have authority over the devil and all the effects of sin, but that we are so far removed from them that it is possible to operate as if they really don't exist.

34) Have a future and hope - Jeremiah 29:11 (NKJV) "For I know the thoughts that I think toward you, says the Lord, thoughts of peace and not of evil, to give you a future and a hope." This is one of our favorite Bible verses, if not our favorite. Like us, maybe you have known deep pain and sorrow in this earthly life. Maybe you have been down so low that you thought recovery was unlikely, and that prosperity was simply out of the question. We have been there, but we know that this verse is true, because we live in the glory of it every day. God has a plan for you. He wants to give you a future, and a hope, and all the blessing you've ever dreamed of. He wants to give you peace, love, companionship, freedom, and victory. Dare to believe this...dare to speak it in faith, and you will see it come to pass in your life on this earth.

The Scriptures mentioned above can be summarized by an explanation of the fact that, at Salvation, you are restored to the same status in which Adam found himself in Genesis 2. Adam was the recipient of the following things: dominion (authority) – Gen. 1:26; seed – Gen. 1:29; made in God's image – Gen. 1:26; having fellowship with God – Gen. 3:8; possessing spiritual life (contact with God) – Gen. 1-3; security – Gen. 2:15; prosperity – Gen. 2:15,16; and perfect health (sickness does not appear in the Bible until Exodus 4 – a result of the fall). Besides all of these, Adam was in partnership with God. In fact, when God gave him dominion over all the earth, Adam was, in truth, God's representative on the earth. God gave Adam the privilege of speaking for Him, and making decisions for Him. God trusted Adam with that responsibility, and he trusts you with that same responsibility. YOU are God's representative on this earth. YOU are His partner on this earth. YOU are His ambassador, and His spokesman, on this earth. He sees you as someone of great worth. To Him, you are far more important than the devil, even far more important than the angels. You are HIS PARTNER.

The ideas that you are insignificant, worthless, or a "throwaway" are simply not true. They are lies initiated by the devil to keep you from realizing "who you are in Christ".

I'd like to close this chapter by borrowing an illustration that I received from a friend. A speaker in a seminar held up a $20 bill. In a room of 200 people, he asked, "Who would like this $20 bill?" Hands went up all over the room. He said, "I will give this $20 to one of you, but first, let me do this." He proceeded to crumple the $20 bill up. He then asked, "Who still wants it?" The hands stayed up in the air. "Well", he replied, "What if I do this?" Then he dropped it on the ground and started to grind it into the floor with his shoe. He picked it up, now crumpled and dirty. "Now, who still wants it?" Dozens of hands eagerly stayed up into the air.

The lesson is clear. People wanted the money because, no matter what had happened to it, it did not decrease in value. It was still worth every bit of $20. My friends, sometimes in this life, we are crushed, thrown to the floor, and ground into the dirt by circumstances that come our way. Because we are human, we tend to feel as though we have become worthless. The lesson of the $20 bill, though, is that no matter what has happened, and no matter what will happen, you will never lose your value in the sight of God. And, you are always priceless to those who love you.

The worth of our lives is not determined by what we do, who we know, or what has happened to us, but by WHO WE ARE IN CHRIST. You are special…don't ever forget that.

Chapter 13

Faith vs. Fear

As a victim of relationship betrayal, and in the middle of your blinding confusion, pain, and disbelief, your enemy, the devil, rushed in to steal certain things from you (John 10:10). He stole your self-esteem, your hope, your plans for the future, and your confidence. You have become afraid of the future, and afraid to trust, at least to some degree.

I don't know the details of your circumstances, but my guess is that you are certainly justified in feeling all the things just mentioned. You probably know, deep in your heart, that they are not the best things for you; not the things that are healthiest for you; and not the kind of things that will lead to healing and victory.

If healing and victory are things that you really want, you will have to do something about fear. It may appear on the surface that fear doesn't even enter the picture, and that you need help with other issues. However, fear is the thing that will hinder your progress toward healing, and can even stop that progress altogether. What is worse, you may not even be aware of the effect of fear in your life.

The goal of this chapter is to move you to a place where you are exercising faith instead of fear. Why is this important? Because faith is the key element in triggering the Lord's blessing in your life. Part of that blessing is healing, restored joy, restored peace, restored confidence, restored hope, and a restored belief that tomorrow will be better.

Without faith, *nothing* can move in the spiritual realm for your good. That is why satan wants you to stay in fear. He'll try to tell you that faith is odd, new, weird, or that it only works sometimes. His goal is to keep you wary of it, so that you will stay in a place where he can continue to mess with your life. You see, he knows that YOU are the one who decides. Satan has no power to keep you in fear. The Lord will not force you into faith. It is entirely your decision.

Our goal, based on our experience, is to convince you to try faith. This information will be based on God's Holy Word, and it has worked for every person who has been willing to try it.

Psalm 118:6 says: "The Lord is on my side; I will not fear." In Psalm 91, we read, "He that dwelleth in the secret place of the Most High shall abide under the shadow of the Almighty. I will say of the Lord, He is my refuge and my fortress; my God; in Him will I trust. Surely He shall deliver thee from the snare of the fowler, and from the noisome pestilence. He shall cover thee with His feathers, and under His wings shalt thou trust; His truth shall be thy shield and buckler. Thou shalt not be afraid for the terror by night; nor for the arrow that flieth by day; nor for the pestilence that walketh in darkness; nor for the destruction that wasteth at noonday. A thousand shall fall at thy side, and ten thousand at thy right hand; but it shall not come nigh thee."

Faith is the key element in triggering the Lord's blessing and the Lord's angels into action. Without faith, *nothing* can move in the spiritual realm for good. Faith—YOUR faith—is the "start" button. It is very much like the key to the ignition of your car. The car will work, and it will take you where you want to go, but you can sit in it all day and get nowhere unless you turn the key.

In the spiritual realm, there exists something that is called a RECIPROCAL. Don't be put off by this word, as it is easily explained. A reciprocal is something that works exactly the same way as something else, but is it's exact opposite. For example, east is the reciprocal of west; up is the reciprocal of down. The reciprocal, or opposite, of faith is fear.

Therefore, FEAR is the key element that triggers satan's cursing and destruction in a life. Satan cannot move in the physical realm unless fear is present, any more than God can move in the physical realm unless faith is present. In short, faith moves God; fear moves satan.

Part 2

I like to go to the Scripture to find my definitions of things, so we'll go to the book of Hebrews 11:1-6 to find the definition of faith. Notice that it says in verse 1, "Now faith is the substance of things hoped for, the evidence of things not seen." In verse 3, we find that "Through faith we understand that the worlds were framed by the Word of God...", and in verse 6, it states that "Without faith, it is impossible to please Him (God)". Verse 1 plainly states that faith can take substance, which means that it can take physical form. Verse 1 also tells us that faith is "the evidence of things not seen". Therefore, we see that faith is a spiritual force. Verse 3 indicates that faith is God's creative power, and the method used to create is words. Lastly, verse 1 says that faith is the substance of things "hoped for".

Fear, as the reciprocal of faith, can be illustrated by the event described in the book of Mark 4:37-40. Those verses tell the story of Jesus and the disciples crossing the Sea of Galilee in a ship. A storm arises and almost sinks the ship. The disciples panic while Jesus sleeps. When they wake him up, He speaks to the storm, and it stops. Then, in verse 40, He says to them, "Why are ye so fearful? How is it that ye have no faith?" From this story, we can see some things about fear. Notice, first of all, that, according to verse 40, the disciples were in fear, not faith. And, they were being destroyed, as the boat was sinking. Fear, therefore, is a spiritual force. Furthermore, it is satan's destructive power, according to verse 38—they were in real fear of their lives. Lastly, in verse 37, it is the evidence of things NOT desired. Please notice how similar fear's characteristics are to those of faith. They are amazingly similar, but have the opposite effect.

Now that we know what faith is, and what fear is, let's look at how they work. First, faith comes by hearing the word of faith (Romans 10:17). Normally, this is a Scripture, or something in line with what Scripture teaches. Secondly, faith is *developed* by meditating on the words that are heard, and then acting upon them. Please do not be put off by my use of the word "meditating". Meditating is a Bible term, and something of great value in developing faith.

SPIRITUAL HEALING

That it has been misused—even abused—by some religious groups does not mean that we should reject it altogether. Meditating means simply thinking about the words of Scripture—the faith words—that were heard. More than that, it means turning it over and over in your mind...even becoming pre-occupied with those words. (The idea here is to implant these positive words of faith and Scripture into your spirit so that they become a part of you.) Thirdly, faith is *applied* by speaking, with your mouth, the truth that the Word of God teaches as though it exists, even though it may not have appeared in the physical realm YET (Romans 4:17; 1 Cor. 1:28). Jesus is the author and developer of faith.

Because fear is the reciprocal (opposite) of faith, it will operate following the same principles. First of all, fear comes by hearing the word—but, in this case, it is the word of the world. We are all exposed to these words every day. The majority of the people around us speak words in line with what they expect from satan's world system (Mark 4:19; Luke 21;25,26). Secondly, fear is developed by meditating on those words. We don't recognize that we meditate on the words of the world because we call this meditating worry; anxiety; or concern. If we meditate sufficiently on these words, we will find ourselves acting in line with those words. Thirdly, we apply fear to our lives by "speaking of things that are not as though they were"—exactly as is stated in Romans 4:17 for faith. For example, we say, "There's a flu bug going around, I just know I'll get it." Or, we say, "I just know that traffic light will turn red for me." Or, we say, "My life will never be happy since this betrayal has happened to me." In countless similar ways, we are reinforcing the words that we have heard in the world, and which we have received into our own heart. In reality, we are simply living in line with what we believe in our heart. Satan is the supporter and developer of fear (remember II Timothy 1:7 – fear is a *spirit*).

It is important that you realize at this point that faith and fear are not only reciprocals, but they are *opposites*. Where one exists, the other *cannot* exist. By way of illustration, if you begin walking east, you are heading east, but no other direction. You can't be going west and east at the same time. However, if you turn around and begin walking the other way, then you are walking west, and cannot be walking east. Our society tends to teach that we can be in faith and fear in varying degrees at the same time. This is not possible, and it is important that you realize that when you are in fear, you are not in faith in any way.

Fear leads to doubt. Doubt ultimately leads to unbelief. It is a process, and an undeniable progression. However, according to I John 4:15-18, fear is not natural to the "new man" that you have become at salvation. Fear, therefore, has to be *received* (like faith) before it can work (like faith). According to Proverbs 4:22; Matthew 14:30; and Psalm 101:3, we receive whatever it is that we continually consider in our heart. What we consider in our heart is a product of what we hear, and what we expose our ears and eyes to. This matter of faith and fear, then, is a heart matter, and the question boils down to "what do you really believe in your heart?" IT WILL SHOW.

The book of Job is traditionally taught to be an instruction manual on the subject "why do the righteous suffer?" This teaching indicates that, although Job was a righteous man, he possessed some hidden imperfections, which God chose to purge out of him by making him suffer. With all due respect to the sincere, Godly people who teach in this way, that is not the essential teaching of the book. In Job 1:5, we read that Job offered burnt offerings for all of his children every day, saying, "It may be that my sons have sinned, and cursed God in their hearts." There is no evidence in the book that his sons had, in fact, done these things, but this is what Job spoke out of his mouth. Furthermore, the same verse says that Job spoke these words *continually* (he is speaking "the word of the world", and is meditating on it by doing so continually). In Job 1 and 2, we are told that satan comes before the Lord and tempts the Lord to persecute Job. In fact, he challenges the Lord to do so (Job 1:9-11). The Lord's response to this challenge is found in Job 1:12 where He says, "Behold, all that he hath is in thy power." Then the Lord limits the scope of satan's attack on Job. Notice, please, that the Lord is not giving permission for satan to attack, but is simply stating a fact—that Job has put himself into a position outside of God's blessing, but within the control and power of satan's realm. How has this happened? It has happened because Job has been speaking and practicing fear with regard to his children and his own life. Job himself admits these things in chapter 3:25. Notice, too, that in Job 6:23, Job is aware that he is suffering at the hands of the devil, not the Lord God. The book of Job teaches us the consequences of speaking and living under the influence of the spirit of fear. Essentially, Job placed himself outside of the realm of God's protection and blessing, and into an area where satan could freely attack him. It was not God's will that this be so, but, as always, the Lord will not impose on a man's free will. It is true that the Lord places limits on what satan can do, but that is an expression of His mercy and grace. In Job 42, which is the last chapter in the book, Job repents of speaking wrongly (Job 42:3), and purposes to live and speak in faith. Once this occurs, the Lord is again in a position to bless Job and does so twice as much as He had before.

What you say—the words that come out of your mouth—are product of what you believe in your heart. Matthew 12:34 says, "Out of the abundance of the heart the mouth speaketh." If you live in the realm of fear and believe that bad things are bound to happen to you, you are allowing the fear system to be at work in your life. As with Job, there will be consequences, because speaking fear (things opposite of the Word of God) places you outside of the Lord's realm of blessing. On the other hand, if your words reflect Scriptural principles, or are in fact the Scriptures themselves, you will train your heart to believe what the Bible says, and you will be living in the realm of faith where God can bless you abundantly.

Fear, when it is acted upon, produces negative things in a person's life (sin and death). Faith, when it is acted upon, produces good things in one's life (abundant life). This is a spiritual law, and it is as unchanging as the law of gravity (Romans 8:2). The term "fear not" appears over sixty times in the Bible. Obviously, it is a matter of choice—YOUR choice. God *cannot* make this choice for you. In other words, stopping fear is an act of the will (II Cor. 10:3-5). In addition, fear has not been given to us (II Timothy 1:7), but faith has been given to us (Romans 12:3). Jesus delivered us from fear (Hebrews 2:14,15). Fear is part of the curse on mankind (Deut. 28:65-67). It is torment, and the worst of the forms of bondage.

James 2:17 says that faith without action is dead. Because that is the Word of God, the reciprocal must also be true—fear without action is dead. And, I John 5:18 indicates that satan can't do anything TO you apart from fear, any more than God can do something FOR you without faith.

An old proverb goes like this: "Fear knocked at the door; Faith answered, and no one was there."

Chapter 14

Traps

The pain of a relationship betrayal can be among the most severe one can experience in this life. It is especially devastating when it involves a long-term relationship, and particularly if vows, promises, and covenants are involved. I described the pain that I felt as being so intense on the inside that I could feel it physically on the outside of my body.

Having unleashed such havoc on a person, you would think that even the devil would say, "Enough." Of course, that's not how his job description reads. He is never content; it never seems to be enough; he can always think of some additional way to bring suffering upon you. In this chapter, we want to briefly list some items that the devil will try to do to keep you in bondage to your pain and suffering. These are things that will occur after the betrayal, and, if you are like most people, you may not see them coming because you are consumed by the struggle to cope with the betrayal.

Some of these items have been mentioned previously, and some have not. They are mentioned here simply to serve as an opportunity for you to prepare for them. Knowing that they will be coming your way will give you opportunity to be watchful for them, and to be prepared to deal with them. These (traps) are:

1. A feeling of worthlessness – It will be difficult not to think of yourself as a "throwaway". Someone who knows you reasonably well considers you to be just that. The idea is to keep you down and defeated. You combat this by re-studying chapter 12 of this book, which deals with who you are in Christ. The only way to defeat this additional attack is to focus on who Jesus Christ says you are, and to remember that His opinion is the most important one—no matter how you feel, and no matter how someone else may feel.

2. Self pity – You are human, and it is inevitable that you will experience many low points. It would be unreasonable, I think, to expect you to live above these. It will not hurt you in the long run to spend a little time feeling sorry for yourself. It's OK to wallow in it for a little while, but only for a little while. Just don't let yourself stay there. Wallow a little, then get up and dust yourself off, and go about the business of living the life that the Lord wants you to live.

3. A feeling of hopelessness – Again, if you're human, some amount of this is unavoidable. A large portion of your life has been exploded, and for a little while, it will look almost hopeless. This is where faith comes in. If there is a God (and there most definitely is), there is hope. If there is hope, there is recovery…healing…even victory. Here is something that has helped others, and might be worth reading over and over again: God says, "Everything will be all right."

4. Fear – If you are a woman, you'll be afraid to trust another man. If you are a man, you'll feel like you can't trust another woman. It will occur to you to be afraid of loneliness. There will be some doubt in your heart about how your financial situation will work out. You will be afraid of even the thought of the "D" word (divorce). Many people are afraid of what others will think. Parents will wonder, "What will happen to the kids?" Although these are all legitimate concerns, the answer lies in chapter 13 of this book, where we learned how faith is the answer to overcoming fear.

5. Anger – You WILL get angry! Actually, that is not as unhealthy or abnormal as you might think. It is another one of those human reactions that is simply a part of the healing process. If you try to suppress the anger, you will do yourself harm. It would be much better to just get it out (in a way that is safe for you and others) and then begin to move away from it. Don't deny it, but most importantly, don't let it get control of you.

6. Replay – One of the nastiest of the traps that satan uses is what I call "replay". I am referring to the process of reliving

past events in our minds—over and over again. We think "I should have said...", or "I could have done..." It's almost as though we can change those events if we just think about them enough. What we're really doing, though, is allowing the devil to hurt us with the same events repeatedly. The event itself was devastating enough, but his goal is to stab us with it as often as possible by having us relive it. It is not easy to forget so devastating an event. Only God Almighty can give us the power to put these things into the background. It will require close communication with Him; lots of time in prayer, but you will find yourself replaying these events less and less.

7. Unforgiveness – Although this is dealt with in depth in the next chapter, your enemy, the devil, knows that an unwillingness to forgive harms YOU more than anyone else, because it keeps you in bondage to that awful past event. After a while, you will come to realize that, very often, the other person involved in the betrayal doesn't know, or even care, whether he or she is forgiven.

Do not be surprised if you experience one or all of these traps. Although satan will use any method he can to continue to hurt you, you can effectively defeat each one through Jesus Christ and His Word. This is something satan does not want you to know. The closer you stay to Jesus and His Word, and the more time you spend with Him, the less effective the devil will be in successfully hurting you with any of these traps.

Chapter 15

How To Forgive

*F*orgiveness is the last and most important step in your journey to spiritual health. One part of you will resist the idea of forgiveness, because your hurt has been deep and has caused unwanted changes, many of which can affect the rest of your life. In this chapter, we will address why you should forgive; what forgiveness is; what forgiveness is not; and some simple steps on how to forgive.

There are several reasons why you should forgive those who have hurt you. The more standard of those include: it is recommended by God (Matthew 6:14,15); and it is recommended as standard procedure among believers (Ephesians 4:31,32). But here is a more compelling reason: it is the *only way* that you can avoid being trapped by satan. Why? Because unforgiveness creates an area of darkness in your spirit—a place where satan can dwell and operate effectively. Therefore, this area of darkness must be avoided so that satan is given no place in which to work (II Corinthians 2:11).

In order to understand what forgiveness is, it is often helpful to begin by revealing what forgiveness is <u>not</u>. Forgiveness is not forgetting. I know that it is common in the world for people to recommend that you "forgive and forget". You may be familiar with the old story about the woman who agreed to bury the hatchet, but vowed to "leave the handle exposed for easy retrieval". I don't recommend that you spend a lot of time trying to forget what has happened because that effort usually leads to failure. I have heard people say that God has forgotten our sins, but it is difficult to understand how that could be if He knows all things. Instead, the Bible teaching is that when we confess, He *separates us* from our sin by determining never to use it against us (Psalm 103:12). You can forgive without forgetting.

You may be saying to yourself, "If I forgive what has been done, I'm allowing that person to get away with what they've done."

But I am not recommending that you become a doormat or a patsy, nor am I recommending even that you tolerate the sin against you. I am not recommending that you run to this person, give them a big hug, and be their best friend. (However, you may, in fact, want to do this. If that's your decision, then that's what you should do.) Our focus in this book is YOU—your relationship with the Lord, and you achieving spiritual freedom for yourself. Whether the other person seeks forgiveness, or repents, is not the focus here. In fact, they may not ever know that you have forgiven them. The focal point here is YOUR freedom and YOUR health. This leads me to an additional point about forgiveness.

Forgiveness does not demand revenge or repayment for offenses. The Word of God says, "Vengeance is Mine; I will repay, saith the Lord" (Romans 12:19). It may help you to understand that the point of this chapter is that your act of forgiveness lets the other person off YOUR hook, but that God doesn't necessarily let them off HIS hook. The issue of their relationship with God depends upon them. Their repentance, and their forgiveness, is a completely different matter, and is actually unrelated to your willingness to forgive. By letting them off your hook, you set yourself free from the pain and from the past, and that is our primary goal here.

I saw an excellent illustration of this principle while watching a church service in Virginia. The preacher asked a man from the congregation to come forward and face him. The preacher placed his hand on the man's shoulder, and said, "This is what it looks like when you have something against another person. Because my hand is touching his shoulder, anything he does will have an effect on me, and anything I do will have an effect on him. Furthermore, we are both limited in our movement. In order for me to move, I must drag him along, and the same is true for him." Then this preacher removed his hand from the man's shoulder and commented, "Now, my hand is no longer in contact with him, or, we could say that I have 'nothing against him'. What he does will not affect me now, and my freedom of movement is restored." This illustration had a powerful effect on me. It was a visual illustration of what I have described above. Your choice to forgive will do you as much good—and probably much more good—than the other person will experience, and you will be free to move away from the person and the circumstances which had previously held you in bondage. That is, forgiveness benefits you because it frees you to move on with your life.

Forgiveness also means resolving, in your own heart, to live with the consequences of the other person's sin. I know that is a difficult sentence to read, because the pain has been intense and you would like to believe that it will all go back to being the way it was before. The truth is that you would have to live with the consequences of sin whether you forgave or not. The good news is that the Lord, through your choice to forgive, will make things right for you. You are His kid!

Let's now address forgiveness itself. I'm going to identify ten steps to forgiveness. As you read these, please keep in mind that you are human—you will experience hurt, pain...even hatred when someone sins against you. The only way to stop the pain and the damage, and to completely heal, is to forgive.

1. Write down the name or names of the people who have offended you. It is important that you see this in written form. In addition, briefly describe the specific wrongs that you feel you have suffered.

2. Face the hurt. On the same list, write down how you feel about what has happened. (It is all right to do this—it is not a sin to recognize the reality of your emotions.)

3. Acknowledge the significance of Calvary. It is the cross that makes forgiveness legally possible and morally right. Remember that Jesus took all sins on Himself at the cross—even those things that were sinned against you. The human side of you will say, "That isn't fair! Where is the justice?" But a loving God has grace enough to cover any and all transgressions. If this were not so, He might not be able to forgive you or me.

4. Decide to pursue a path of meekness, grace, and restoration. That is, determine within yourself that you will not retaliate in the future (Galatians 6:1,2).

5. Decide to forgive. Forgiveness is a matter of the will. It is a choice. In this case, you are making a choice to free yourself from the past. More than likely, you will not feel like doing this. Fortunately, it isn't a matter of how you feel. You can still choose to forgive even though you may not feel like doing so. Remember, this choice has nothing to do with whether or not the other person did wrong. That is not the issue in this case. The issue is your willingness to free them from your hook.

6. Take your list to God. Set it before Him and pray—out loud (so that you can hear it), "Lord, I forgive _____ for _____." Do this with each person and each offense. It will be extremely difficult to do. It is most often done through tears, but they will very shortly be tears of joy.

7. Destroy the list. Why? Because the Lord has set you free from each person and each offense. The list is of no value any longer. You are set free from it, just as surely as the preacher was set free when he removed his hand from the man's shoulder in our previous example.

8. Do not expect your forgiveness to cause change in the other person or persons. In fact, they're probably not even aware that you have prayed. We often expect that our generous forgiveness will cause a noticeable change in others, or that somehow the Lord will cause them to change. But it is YOU who prayed. It is YOU who has been changed. Your prayer has set YOU free.

9. Expect your forgiveness to cause positive results in you. The hurt will fade; your anger will diminish; your resentment of past circumstances will decrease. In their place you will begin to experience strength, joy, freedom, relief, and a renewed closeness with your Father God.

PART 2

10. Thank Jesus for the growth you have enjoyed through these experiences. Satan's goal from the beginning was to do you harm. Forgiveness is the tool that God uses to turn the tables on the devil, and to use those same circumstances to strengthen the believer. You are no longer a victim; you are no longer in pain; you are no longer a person hurt in ways that will never go away. You are strong now, and you can sense it in your spirit. You are a blessed child of God, and your choice to forgive has given you total victory and healing.

In the list of people that you wrote in item 2 above, did you remember two important names? Many people forget to list: 1) themselves – if you consider your circumstances carefully, you might find that, in some ways, you were blaming yourself for what happened. Choose to forgive yourself...Jesus has. 2) Jesus Himself – search your heart and you might find a part of it that clings to the possibility that Jesus had something to do with what happened. He didn't, but you wouldn't be any less than human if you thought so. You need to release Him—and yourself—from those feelings.

My dear brother or sister, you are NOT locked in the past. You do NOT have to live with the pain of a former event forever. The person you are is NOT determined by your circumstances. The person you are is NOT determined by satan. The person you are is NOT determined by someone who did a terrible wrong to you. Forgiveness has set you free from all of these, and allowed you to live in the reality that you are God's child. The person you are IS determined by who God says you are, and who His Word says you are. Believe that, and be encouraged by it. You are valued, precious, righteous, strong, pure, useful, and FREE! Your willingness to forgive has released you from bondage, and has been a mighty defeat for our enemy, the devil.

TO FORGIVE IS TO SET THE PRISONER FREE ...
AND THEN DISCOVER THE PRISONER WAS YOU

Chapter 16

How to Pray Effectively

The betrayal you have endured and the ensuing pain may be the worst thing that has ever happened to you in your life. Hopefully, the coping methods and means to spiritual healing described in the previous chapters will give you strength to take the steps necessary to begin to restore your injured spirit. In Chapter 14, we talked to you about traps the devil will set in order to keep you in pain, confusion, and uncertainty about your life, especially in regard to the betrayal. God's will for you is to be released from the pain satan delights in inflicting. Although it may be difficult for you to believe this right now, time will pass and the pain WILL begin to lessen.

If you have taken to heart the messages of hope contained in the previous chapters, and if you allow yourself to take the steps to forgiveness, the Lord will free you from the aching within your spirit. However, YOU play an important part in this healing process. Did you know that God Himself has given us a means not only to endure, but to triumph over the trials of this world? It is the Bible—the Word of God. He has revealed it to men who have recorded His directives in the most important book ever written. The Bible contains the God-ordained way to navigate through this life. While on this earth, we are living in satan's home turf. Problems, pain, loneliness, lack, sickness—satan delights in throwing it all our way. What he counts on is that you will become discouraged and give up. What he doesn't want you to know is that God has made a way for you to conquer "satan's fiery arrows", and that way is to pray effectively—according to Scripture.

In Chapter 2, "Give Yourself to God", I described how I threw myself completely into the arms of God when I learned of my ex-husband's betrayal. Because I already had a relationship with the Lord, this was a natural response for me. Although at that time

Part 2

in my life I was a Christian, I was not a Bible reader. Had I been, it would not have taken as long for me to recover from the betrayal and subsequent divorce. I have since learned how important reading, believing, and speaking the actual WORDS OF GOD is. Because I believed God did not cause the breakup of my marriage, my faith led me to believe God had the restoration of my spirit in His will. I have since learned, also, that speaking FAITH is what activates the power of God. And faith comes from hearing—hearing from the Word of God. The most important part of the restoration of my spirit was beginning to read the Bible.

One day, a friend gave me a little pamphlet on how to read the Bible in a year. It provided direction on what chapters and verses to read each day. I saw it as an opportunity to learn, but little did I realize how life-changing that opportunity would be. The Bible compares faith to a mustard seed—starting tiny, but with the capability of becoming huge. How does it grow? First of all by planting it. Then by tending to it. I tended to my "seed" (faith) by beginning to read the Word of God. As I read, the Spirit of God began to reveal simple truths to me. Most importantly, I became convinced that God loves me. He has ONLY goodness in store for me. All of the other things ("badness", if you will) come NOT from God. Well then, where do the "bad things" come from? From God's enemy, and our enemy, satan.

Reading the Bible opens the eyes of your spirit. Gradually, passages that once seemed to make little sense become plain. Through Scripture, God reveals His will, His ways, His plans. II Timothy 2:15 tells us, "Study to show yourself approved." By studying the Bible, we show God we want to learn His ways, His will, His plans. The Bible tells us HOW to combat satan's attacks. James 4:7 tells us, "Submit yourselves to God. Resist the devil and he will *flee* from you." Once I learned that wonderful news, I began to search God's Word for passages that would make me victorious over satan. Little by little, certain passages began to speak to me. I wrote them in my journal so that my favorite, most meaningful Scriptures would be readily available to me. I try to read them every day. I read them out loud, so that satan can hear my profession of faith. They are God's Words of encouragement, hope, promise, and victory.

A most important part of God's plan for you to walk in victory involves your commitment to walking "righteously". You can't pick and choose which parts of the Bible you intend to believe and follow. ALL the words of the Bible are right and true. And God's will for us is to live "righteously". Proverbs 3:7,8 says "Fear the Lord and shun evil; this will bring health to your body and nourishment to your bones." Does fear mean we are to "be afraid" of God? No, fear means hear, obey, and reverence. God is love, and in response to that love, we will want to know His ways and walk in His will. The Bible will reveal to you how to walk in His ways.

The Appendix of this book contains some of my favorite Scripture passages. It is my hope that they will be a source of comfort and hope to you. Read them, out loud if you can. Let the devil know that YOU know he is a defeated enemy! It is news he dreads hearing. Now you can begin to take a stand against his wiles and attacks. How wonderful it is to know that whatever assault satan takes against you, God has provided you with a defense. Read below the description of the "armor of God"… it is our assurance that satan CANNOT win. He can try, and he will; but God is on our side. God's Word is supreme! Your seed of faith, now planted, can begin to grow. However, just as a seed planted in a garden takes time and nourishment to grow, it is not instantaneous. It takes patience until you see the results. Become convinced in your heart that God's way is the only way. Satan will try to convince you to stop watering your seed, to neglect your garden, to give up. Outsmart him! Be patient, but diligent. There is a divine order to things. This is especially true where spiritual things are concerned. Have faith…plant it…nourish it in God's Word…BELIEVE, and KEEP BELIEVING that you will receive "the harvest"—God's goodness!

The Scriptures listed in the Appendix are verses from God's Word that may help you to begin to see that God wants GOOD THINGS for you. He NEVER inflicts pain, poverty, sickness, loneliness, fear, or any other bad thing upon you. He has made a way for us to remain under His protection…and that way is to speak Scripture when we pray. Luke 11:28 says, "…blessed are they that hear the word of God and keep it." Do you want to be blessed? Do you want to be an overcomer? Do you want to stand strong against any problems the future holds? You need more than physical sustenance to live this life on earth. Matthew 4:4 tells us that, "Man shall not live by bread alone, but by every word that proceeds out of the mouth of God." Find a verse of Scripture that agrees with your prayer request; believe it in your heart and speak it with your mouth. Be patient, hopeful, and faithful. Become convinced that God's Words are the source of victory.

If you are a Christian, at some point in the past you have made Jesus Christ the Lord of your life. However, there may be some of you reading this book who do not have a relationship with God and His Son, our Savior, Jesus Christ. Perhaps you are not a Christian, and you have no idea what this Christianity is all about. God sent His only Son, Jesus, to be born on this earth, to suffer and die on the cross for our sins, and to be raised from the dead. His death and resurrection paid for our sinfulness. He paved the way for us to receive eternal blessings and happiness for all eternity with God.

Is this some rite that is reserved for a chosen few? No, Jesus died to save ALL. Acts 16:30,31 says, "…what must I do to be saved? Believe on the Lord Jesus Christ and thou shalt be saved." Jesus Himself said "Behold, I stand at the door and knock: if any man hear my voice, and open the door, I will come in to him" (Revelation 3:20).

Open the door to Jesus. He loves you and has paid the way for you to have everlasting life with Him. Give your life to Him… it will be the best decision you have ever made. Receive Him into your heart as you speak the following words:

> "Heavenly Father, I believe that your Son, Jesus Christ, died for my sin. By faith I now receive Jesus into my heart as my Savior; I trust Him for the salvation of my soul. I make Jesus the Lord of my

life. Help me, Lord, to do your will each day. In Jesus' name I pray. Amen."

If you spoke these words with your mouth and believed them in your heart, you are now a child of God, and the angels are rejoicing in heaven at this very moment. Whatever has happened to you in the past is past. You have opened the door and let Jesus into your life. You never have to experience loneliness again. Find a fellow Christian and share your good news with him/her. If you have no one with whom to share your news, please contact us, and we will rejoice with you and give you some guidance on how to begin your walk in the abundant life Jesus died to purchase for you. You are now free, forgiven, and victorious. Praise God!

Now that you are a Christian, or if you have been a Christian before this time, you know that the healing and restoration you have been seeking is already in place. Our God, who IS love, has declared in His Word that this is so. You want to insure that you experience these things for yourself, and in this regard, it is important that you understand that you have a part to play. The Lord has made us, as saved Christians, partners with Him in the faith process. His is the larger and more difficult part—He has won the victory over our enemy that makes our healing and restoration a spiritual fact.

Our responsibility is to believe that these things are true, and to speak and pray in absolute faith that they are so. Speaking Scripture in faith is the spiritual equivalent of planting seed, and it is God's basic method of operation in His kingdom. Every promise in Scripture is already established in the spiritual realm because God's Word has to be true. The part we play is to move those spiritual truths from the spiritual realm into the physical realm so that they become a reality in our earthly life. The operation that causes this to happen is for God's children to have enough faith in the truth of His Words to speak them as if they were already true in the physical realm (Romans 4:17).

It is through this method that you will, over time, experience the mending of your broken heart, and a strengthening of your love and bond with the Lord, Jesus Christ. He loves you. He experiences

PART 2

your pain, and desires for you to be healed, restored, and happy. Your willingness to work with Him by simply applying your faith to His Word will accomplish that result. It is truly a miracle, but it is one that we know by experience can and will occur.

We rejoice with you in advance for the full recovery you will experience, and for the abundance of blessings that our generous God has in store for you. Your life has not ended—in the best of ways, it has only just begun.

Jeremiah 29:11 (NKJV)
"For I know the thoughts that I think toward you, says
the Lord, thoughts of peace and not of evil,
to give you a future and a hope."
(God wants only good things for us.)

Appendix

Scripture Verses Of Encouragement And Hope

The Armor of God
"...Be strong in the Lord, and in the power of his might. Put on the whole armour of God, that ye may be able to stand against the wiles of the devil. For we wrestle not against flesh and blood, but against principalities, against powers, against the rulers of the darkness of this world, against spiritual wickedness in high places. Wherefore take unto you the whole armour of God, that ye may be able to withstand in the evil day, and having done all, to stand. Stand therefore, having your loins girt about with truth, and having on the breastplate of righteousness; and your feet shod with the preparation of the gospel of peace; above all, taking the shield of faith, wherewith ye shall be able to quench all the fiery darts of the wicked. And take the helmet of salvation, and the sword of the Spirit, which is the Word of God: praying always with all prayer and supplication in the Spirit..." (Ephesians 6:10-18).

"He shall not be afraid of evil tidings: his heart is fixed, trusting in the Lord. His heart is established, he shall not be afraid..." (Psalm 112:7,8).

"We walk by faith, not by sight" (II Corinthians 5:7). (I am not moved by what I see or feel. I am moved by the Word of God, and I call it <u>done</u>, in Jesus' Name.)

"Seek ye first the kingdom of God and His righteousness, and all these things shall be added unto you" (Matthew 6:33).

"I sought the Lord, and He heard me, and delivered me from all my fears" (Psalm 34:4).

"Fear thou not; for I am with thee: be not dismayed; for I am thy God: I will strengthen thee; yea, I will help thee; yea, I will uphold thee with the right hand of My righteousness" (Isaiah 41:10).

APPENDIX

"Be strong and of a good courage; be not afraid, neither thou be dismayed; for the Lord thy God is with thee withersoever thou goest" (Joshua 1:9). (Faith in God's Word is being courageous.)

"Be not overcome of evil, but overcome evil with good" (Romans 12:21). (Satan has no power over me when I overcome evil with good.)

"No weapon that is formed against thee shall prosper...this is the heritage of the servants of the Lord" (Isaiah 54:17).

"Trust in the Lord with all thine heart; and lean not unto thine own understanding. In all thy ways acknowledge Him, and He shall direct thy paths" (Proverbs 3:5,6).

"Blessed be the Lord, because He hath heard the voice of my supplications. The Lord is my strength and my shield; my heart trusted in Him, and I am helped" (Psalm 28:6,7).

"Submit yourselves therefore to God. Resist the devil and he will flee from you" (James 4:7) (This is GOOD news).

"The Lord is gracious, and full of compassion, slow to anger and of great mercy. The Lord is good to all; and His tender mercies are over all His works" (Psalm 145:8,9). (The Lord wants me to be well and happy.)

"I will say of the Lord, He is my refuge and my fortress; my God; in Him will I trust" (Psalm 91:2). (I claim my place in God's protection.)

"He (the man established in righteousness) shall not be afraid of evil tidings; his heart is fixed, trusting in the Lord" (Psalm 112:7).

"The work of righteousness shall be peace; and the effect of righteousness quietness and assurance forever" (Isaiah 32:17). (I want to receive your peace, Lord.)

"Surely He shall deliver thee from the snare of the fowler, and from the noisome pestilence. He shall cover thee with His feathers, and under His wings shalt thou trust; His truth shall be thy shield and buckler" (Psalm 91:3,4). (I am safe in God's hands.)

"Let all those that put their trust in Thee rejoice; let them ever shout for joy, because Thou defendest them… for Thou, Lord, wilt bless the righteous; with favor wilt Thou compass them as with a shield" (Psalm 5:11,12).

"Yea, though I walk through the valley of the shadow of death, I will fear no evil; for Thou art with me" (Psalm 23:4).

"The hope of the righteous shall be gladness…the way of the Lord is strength to the upright" (Proverbs 10:28,29).

"Brethren, whatsoever things are true…honest…just…pure…lovely…of good report…think on these things" (Philippians 4:8). (Positive words allow the goodness of God to be activated.)

"My God shall supply all your need according to His riches in glory by Christ Jesus" (Philippians 4:19).

"The Lord will be a refuge for the oppressed, a refuge in times of trouble. And they that know Thy Name will put their trust in Thee; for Thou, O Lord, hast not forsaken them that seek Thee" (Psalm 9:9,10).

"I will praise Thee, O Lord, with my whole heart; I will show forth all Thy marvelous works. I will be glad and rejoice in Thee; I will sing praise to Thy name, O Thou most High" (Psalm 9:1,2). (When I praise the Lord, the devil FLEES!!)

"Many there be which say… there is no help for him in God. But Thou, O Lord, art a shield for me; my glory, and the lifter up of mine head" (Psalm 3:2-3). (I believe that You are there for me, Lord.)

APPENDIX

"Many are the afflictions of the righteous, but the Lord delivereth him out of them all" (Psalm 34:19).

"My soul, wait thou only upon God; for my expectation is from Him. He only is my rock and my salvation; He is my defence; I shall not be moved" (Psalm 62:5,6). (Have patience)

"And let us not be weary in well doing; for in due season we shall reap, if we faint not" (Galatians 6:9). (Don't give up…God will come through)

"Therefore, I will look unto the Lord; I will wait for the God of my salvation; my God will hear me" (Micah 7:7).

"The Lord shall guide thee continually, and satisfy thy soul in drought, and make fat thy bones; and thou shalt be like a watered garden, and like a spring of water, whose waters fail not" (Isaiah 58:11). (My seed of faith will grow in my garden, watered by the Word of God)

"I can do all things through Christ which strengtheneth me" (Philippians 4:13). (Hang on…it's not "if", it's "when")

"They that wait upon the Lord shall renew their strength; they shall mount up with wings as eagles; they shall run, and not be weary; and they shall walk, and not faint" (Isaiah 40:31).

"For God hath not given us the spirit of fear, but of power and of love, and of a sound mind" (2 Timothy 1:7).

"Thou wilt keep him in perfect peace, whose mind is stayed on Thee, because he trusteth in Thee" (Isaiah 26:3).

"…No good thing will He withhold from them that walk uprightly" (Psalm 84:11).

"Let not your heart be troubled, neither let it be afraid" (John 14:27). (The devil cannot get to me if I refuse to be afraid)

"Whoso hearkeneth unto Me shall dwell safely, and shall be quiet from fear of evil" (Proverbs 1:33).

"The Lord giveth wisdom: out of His mouth cometh knowledge and understanding. He layeth up sound wisdom for the righteous; He is a buckler to them that walk uprightly. He keepeth the paths of judgment, and preserveth the way of His saints" (Proverbs 2:6-8) .

"Turn not from it (God's Word) to the right hand or to the left, that thou mayest prosper withersoever thou goest" (Joshua 1:7).

…"Choose you this day whom ye will serve…but as for me and my house, we will serve the Lord" (Joshua 24:15).

"Casting all your care upon Him, for He careth for you" (1 Peter 5:7).

"For He shall give His angels charge over thee, to keep thee in all thy ways" (Psalm 91:11).

"The Name of the Lord is a strong tower; the righteous runneth into it, and is safe" (Proverbs 18:10). (I am safe in YOU, Lord)

"Giving thanks unto the Father…who hath delivered us from the power of darkness, and hath translated us into the kingdom of His dear Son" (Colossians 1:12-13).

"Eye hath not seen, nor ear heard, neither have entered into the heart of man, the things God hath prepared for them that love Him" (1 Corinthians 2:9).

"…Whoso trusteth in the Lord, happy is he" (Proverbs 16:20).

"I will both lay me down in peace, and sleep: for Thou, Lord, only maketh me dwell in safety" (Psalm 4:8).

"For Thou wilt light my candle: the Lord my God will enlighten my darkness" (Psalm 18:28).

Healing For Your Broken Heart is available at:

olivepresspublisher.com

amazon.com

barnesandnoble.com

and other websites.

The E-book is available at:

amazon.com

Book stores and book distributors may obtain this book through:

Ingram Book Company
or by e-mailing

olivepressbooks@gmail.com

Lyn and Jim Kirkland have been writing, teaching, and doing ministry for many years. To schedule them to speak or lead a seminar contact:

Starfish Ministries of Pennsylvania

www.starfishofpa.com

info@starfishofpa.com

(717) 201 - 1514

The name "Starfish" comes from the story of a boy saving starfish one at a time on a seashore. When told that he was not making a difference among the thousands of stranded starfish on the beach, he quickly responded, "It made a difference to that one."

The goal of Starfish Ministries is to "give hope and comfort to hurting souls in the Body of Christ."

www.ingramcontent.com/pod-product-compliance
Lightning Source LLC
Chambersburg PA
CBHW060211050426
42446CB00013B/3053